Ded

For Wendy and Kim

and

In memory of a Dear Departed Friend who saw me
at my worst but encouraged me in relentless pursuit
of walking again. Rufus, my lurcher, stayed with me
from 50 yards in an hour to 8 mile walks a day - his
encouragement had that startling effect created by
unconditional love.

Contents

Acknowledgements

It always gives joy to say Thank You and it always brings hope when others help.

Life is strange, for the first person to whom I owe such enormous gratitude is my late wife Wendy, who suffered in silence my initial berating of the system, offered unrelenting help while transcribing my illegible scrawl and then encouraged me with my struggle, as I shrugged off the terminal diagnosis in favour of a prolonged useful life. Then all those fellow sufferers who found strength from reading my story, which gave me in turn strength to help. When I did not die I was oft heard to say "what now may I do with my life." Cancer - A Strange Gift is just that, the answer I hope to helping others.

It is, with the utmost joy that I say Thank You Marilyn, a friend with whom much has been shared over many years but none so much as your endless help, encouragement, support, guidance, patience, not to mention editing, all of which Marilyn you have suffered for me over the last year, and without which this story would not have been published. I say Thank You with all my heart for that help which in turn will, I hope, help others.

Meeting Leyla added that 'je ne sais quoi', without which I would have neither title nor the 'Map' - of life. I say to you also, Thank You so much for your interest, and for the far reaching input of your artistic and holistic mind's insight into the transformation of a troubled patient's mindset from worry to freedom, to pursue with renewed strength the positivity of life and the future. I, and those who read my book, are forever indebted for your far reaching thinking and help.

And an enormous Thank You to Colin, you are the first person to read the final draft, your constructive and creative input is invaluable, Thank You.

Claire, Thank You also for being that friend from within the system, who knew all and helped me with your knowledge and strength and your wonderfully supportive written words.

For the wider issues and understanding of the complementary scenario; Anne, Thank You for the wonderful debate, help, sincerity and support - not to mention your written words also. You have been a wonderful ear over many years with the ultimate wisdom of one who knows all too well the need for support from wherever it may come, when the body and the mind are in crisis, I so Thank You for you.

Then, finally, Michael - My Chinaman!. My Dear Friend, without you I am sure that I would not now be sitting remembering, recalling the trauma of mind and, through your intense encouragement, striving to find MY positivity which enabled me to see the 'NOW' and then life's future . The 'NOW' is more than twenty years on, my doctor has retired, as also has my oncologist -they could not stand the strength you gave me, nor the pace ! THANK YOU.

Foreword

I have known John, and his wife Wendy before her passing, for some twenty years. He is a man of great distinction and many talents, from being a CEO to a down-to-earth family man. He has travelled the globe extensively, is the kindest, most generous, man I have had the good fortune to meet, and has helped me by giving advice when I have needed it; I find him most inspiring.

I have worked in the medical field for some thirty years now, starting as a carer to being a Head of Unit manager, with degrees in nursing, including Pharmacology, Palliative Care and Surgical Procedures. So to be asked to review this forthcoming book was indeed a great honour for me.

I have read John's book, and agree very strongly with him that alternative complementary medicine can, and does, enhance Western medicine. John's story is pure living proof of this; it shows great tenderness, concerns and determination to survive as he continued his uphill struggle with a great sense of humour.

As stated in his book, it's very true that each of us needs the basic of Self- Help to remain positive, and take part in every aspect of our own care. To embrace it, to research it, to look at other forms of medicine, other than standard Western medicine.

John speaks of treating the cause not the symptoms, which often happens on a daily basis. As individuals we need to educate, and understand what is happening to our very precious bodies, as John did on his journey.

Traditional complementary medicine is heavily rooted in traditional Eastern philosophy but did not originate in only one era of Chinese history. It was built on, added to and modified throughout history. This is very typical of the Chinese people who are very pragmatic, have no problem accepting a wide variety of philosophies into their culture, and do not see any conflict between them. We could learn so much from them, thus enhancing and embracing our own lives.

So much has changed since the last World Health Organisation (WHO) global strategy document, released in 2002. More and more countries are coming to accept the contributions that TCM can make to the health and wellbeing of individuals, and the comprehensiveness of their care systems.

The WHO has a recognised Traditional Medicine Strategy (2002-2005). The updated strategy for the period (2014-2023) devotes more attention than its predecessor to health services and systems including TCM, (Chinese medicine practice, products and practitioners) thus bringing Western and Eastern medicine together. "*TCM being one of the world's oldest medical systems with remote antiquity and opulent contents.*"(quoted from 'A historical overview of traditional Chinese medicine and ancient Chinese medical ethics ' by Cai Jingfeng)

John shows in his book how both types of medicine have benefited his wellbeing. It's a book I will gladly encourage my patients to read and all should take a look at it - there is something for everyone.

Annette Goodfellow

Head of Unit Manager, Barchester Healthcare

Preface

May and June 1998 was the last time I put pen to paper. All was good and I wanted to publish history after prolonging my nine month shortened life expectancy, as asserted by the Western system. I wanted to get a 'story of hope' to others often affected by the negativity of the Western system's statistical tally, which appears so important as a diagnostic prediction.

I could find no publisher and no route to someone who might help me source this outlet from obscurity. I gave up. Then in 1999 I travelled to New Zealand and Australia ostensibly to say goodbye to friends, believing the journey would be fraught. The journey in fact was easy, and from that time on I started to travel extensively again. In 2001, I happened upon an opportunity to fund a stem-cell research company. It was another learning curve for me which took me back to Australia frequently. It also recreated the start of my opine for distrust of the pharmaceutical industry, over and above that which I had already occasioned as a result of my own medical experience. Although she travelled with me during the early stages of 2001, it was at this time also that Wendy, my wife, became ill. Wendy lost weight and had developed a lump on her side. We went to see our doctor and several others as well, I was convinced it was cancer. We were told that it was not.

I will not evidence detail on her case history, but simply say that in March 2005 Wendy was diagnosed with kidney cancer and given six weeks to live. Wendy died in her sleep 9 April 2005 at home in her room, just short of her 59th birthday. Exactly the six weeks after the initial prognosis. For all her misgivings in 1995 about my dying before her, she managed not to have to live alone without me! It is a sanguine reflection upon Western medicine diagnosis; I was given nine months in 1995 and am still here and Wendy, being undiagnosed for 4 years, was given 6 weeks to live after the eventual acceptance that she not only had cancer, but its discovery was so late that it had spread throughout her body. Over her last year of life I repeatedly implored the medical profession to find out where the cancer was situated. The answer, after the event, was that they had repeatedly tested for liver and lung cancer but never kidney. In 2005 I was left a widower, but I had a new research company into which I could pour my energy and remorse.

All was well with my health. I would see Michael, my herbalist, every six weeks or so and touch not a drop of Western medicine in pill or liquid form. My immune system was superlative; colds, coughs, flu, I succumbed to none. I became aware through an obscure article, that most of us who have had radiotherapy have some lasting after effects and some experience new primary tumours.

I sought to ensure that I had my annual MRI scan, in the hope that this would show up any abnormalities at an early stage. The NHS were not very pro the concept for they said that my tumour was still there but dormant; my oncologist was adamant that new primaries from old radiotherapy scar tissues were unlikely. That may or may not be true but in May 2011, I was diagnosed with another primary! It was within an area of scar tissue damage. The detail of anxiety, trauma and operations, is not relevant. The cancer was penile so they cut it off!! All was and still is well five years on. What is not well, is that had I been circumcised after the old radiotherapy tissue damage as I'd wanted, the cancer would have been detected earlier and maybe, not so much would have had to be cut off, and it might not have spread to some lymph nodes necessitating more surgery.

Why is the patient not allowed to express his thoughts to a listening Western ear? Why when antibiotics are given, does the doctor not tell the patient to replace bacteria by eating yogurt? Why is the Western system and practice so opposed to allowing patient input and medical understanding of a better diagnostics, less statistically driven with, if appropriate, the suggestion to the patient that they may like to explore complementary scenarios; as in my case Traditional Chinese Medicine (TCM).

The greater the patient's ability and allowability to explore their own case and take part in their own care, surely greater is their ability to have the power of positive thought. To neglect that ability of soul and spirit and conscious determination negates a whole scenario of patient care. If, as a patient, all you do is visit your GP, take a pill and wait to see what happens, then that patient cannot take active participation in their wellbeing. Self-Help is vital to Helping-Hope.

The Basics of Self-Help

The power of positive thought.

Take part in your care.

Ensure the immune system is effective.

Embrace your illness; don't be afraid.

If you take antibiotics; eat yogurt.

Clare Abbott in the following passage introduces my 'story of hope'.

The Story of Hope

I first met Johnnie in about 2005, when he was still careful about diet and drinking his herbal tea, (this did not prevent him, as a gentleman. eating every scrap of the steak I cooked for him, before I knew it was not allowed). At the time I had little faith in any form of complementary medicine, though I had taken both my sons to the chiropractor with good results. I felt that homeopathy in particular, and other kinds in general, probably worked by the placebo effect - none the worse for that really, as long as patients consulted Western doctors as well. This attitude was the consequence of being a scientist by training and a medical information officer by profession. I worked in the Churchill Library, not many feet away from where Johnnie met his oncologist, at the same time he was receiving his radiotherapy.

I was aware of the controversy surrounding the Bristol Cancer Help Centre, now named after its founder Penny Brohn who defied her prognosis for 20 years. The medical profession had investigated the work of this place in the early 1990s and concluded that people who had been treated there died sooner than those treated by conventional doctors. The harm this report did was incalculable, taking hope -and support- from those who had trusted the Centre. The criticism, which followed its publication, led to the suicide of one of its most eminent authors (Professor Tim McElwain). To this day, the report is held up as an example of how not to do research.

However, in spite of much effort there is very little scientific and unchallengeable evidence that some branches of complementary medicine work at all. I am thinking in particular of homeopathy where the 'active' ingredients are sometimes so diluted that there can be few, if any, molecules of them in the small bottles of 'medicine' as purchased. I am still fairly contemptuous of this, but with the important proviso that anything at all which the patient feels is helping is to be encouraged.

These days Western medicine is evidence-based (randomised double-blind controlled clinical trials), rather than history-based ("it's always been done this way") or anecdote-based ("that's how Bloggs does it"). I have read articles in the 'Journal of Alternative Medicine' which are either risible or horrifying. Some of the authors had no acceptable evidence whatsoever for their assertions. One investigation I remember, into the effect on leucocytes of radiation from mobile phones, used exactly one phone, and not in any samples of leucocytes.

I have no idea whether or not Traditional Chinese Medicine is evidence based, and I rather suppose it is not. It does not matter, except that it has occasionally been shown to cause harm. This is very minimal compared with the iatrogenic disease and death caused by Western medicine every year, 462 deaths recorded as being from complications of medical or surgical care in 2009. Johnnie's Chinaman gave him hope, put him back in control, gave him a diet that would probably be good for all of us (though I have trouble with the Hay concept) and prescribed a herbal remedy. His secondary tumour, said to kill him within a year, became encapsulated, which it still is. I have witnessed for myself that his oncologist (who, naturally enough, I knew professionally) no longer dismisses TCM as he once did.

But the thrust of this book is that the situation is not either/or. You can and should have both kinds of treatment, or at the very least have a choice. These days patients can generally go to a Maggie's centre (within the hospital where they were diagnosed) where, in direct contrast to Johnnie's experience, there may be a beautiful garden, some fresh air, a support specialist with whom to talk things over. The only time I visited a Maggie's Centre, some complementary therapy was on offer. I think the war is at least partly won, and the medical profession is slowly changing. I recently hurt myself quite badly, in ways I don't think TCM can help, but my consultant provided model patient care, even saying to me last time I saw him "You're in the driving seat".

When my mother was a pharmacist working with general practitioners in the years before she married in 1939 (because, oh best-beloved, in those days a professional woman could not practice after marriage even though "there's a war coming, Miss Davison",) a doctor's job was not only to cure sometimes - there were then only six useful drugs in the whole pharmacopoeia!- but to comfort, always. The comfort dimension is very rarely provided in Western medicine today, because we do not value it or because we cannot pay for it. Complementary medicine seems to me to provide much of what we leave out, at the very least.

Johnnie's cancer story does not end with the secondary, as you will read. Whatever your conclusions may be, you cannot help but be impressed with his courage and determination. I still am.

Clare Abbott

Oxford 2012

Cancer Diagnosed

I do not believe that I am alone in the world in living for the future; future hopes, dreams, aspirations and plans; while attempting to enjoy the present. Some days are passed in mundane fashion, some are exciting, some positively encourage realization for the future, while some conversely encourage a defeatist attitude. But always there is tomorrow. Of course as I cross the street I regard the bus, but who doesn't?

Death was at first frightening, something that as a young man was as awful to consider as the simple ageing process. As year followed year, and the milometer began to have 2's, then 3's and 4's in front of the unit, I dreaded each birthday in the knowledge, not that I was nearer death, but that I was no longer young. Youthful prowess was giving way to mature wisdom. The former I relished, the latter seemed always mundane and without quantifiable benefit. To be able to lift a heavy stone, to run a quick mile, to hit a ball with all force produced instantaneous results and personal satisfaction at a job well done. To have to use cunning and guile, wisdom and prolonged thought to contemplate how to move that stone, and how to jump clear when it failed to respond appropriately; to know that a mile was too far to run and that the co-ordination of eye and muscle could result in a miss-hit ball were not the sort of daily success for which I strived. But there was always the morrow.

Then, in the autumn of 1993 I was told that I had cancer of the bowel and that a length of my intestine would need to be removed. An anxiety was instilled in my mind, but the consultant was pretty confident of success. So the morrow, though maybe in doubt, was in no way lost for the future. During the twelve months following the operation, I was often heard to wonder "Why me? Why should I be so lucky to be cured?" The thought was reinforced in my mind as a brave friend in France, spent the same year battling against breast cancer with indomitable courage and a fierce determination to overcome the disease that was truly awe inspiring. At the end of the year after the operation, when the consultant expressed himself well pleased with his handiwork, fears for my fallibility and the morrow began to recede and I felt able to plan again with confidence for the future. Even if such planning was tempered with the realization that each day held more importance than hitherto, and that plans and dreams needed to be forced along rather than be allowed to drift in roughly the right direction. The familiar truism that 'today is the first day of the rest of one's life' had taken on new significance.

Then, on Friday 1st September 1995, the first day of the rest of my life suddenly became the first day of the last year of my life. An oncologist, whom until that day I'd never heard of or set eyes on before, pronounced in response to my questions that he thought he could guarantee me a year of life, after that there would be no hope, no more tomorrows, no more todays to dance. Just 365 days left. I was 52 years old.

I was born of a mother whose lineage can be traced back many hundreds of years. This gave me an enduring interest in history, a perspective of the past and an enquiring mind. My father strived to trace his family back beyond the late eighteenth century without success, but he brought a certain wealth to the partnership which enabled them to send me, as was the custom, to a boarding school from the age of nine onwards.

(Prep school: pneumonia)

The motto of the public school I subsequently attended was 'sapiens qui prospicit'. 'Wise is the man who thinks ahead'. This credo formally lodged itself in my mind at a very early stage. Maybe it was responsible, more than most things, for moulding my life. I liked to plan, I did not like to be caught out by events of which I'd not thought. To this day I still don't, as we try and weave our way through the cut and thrust of modern business, most of our time is spent in forward planning and both Wendy and I find ourselves quoting the Latin as we try and forward guess what life and commerce is likely to throw at us next.

Apart from the influence of the motto, I strived during my public school days for diversification, primarily on the sports field, since the academic world did not hold the same attractions! I was not content to run in just the mile, I wished and did represent the school at the quarter and half mile as well. In fact, I represented the school in most sports at some stage during my stay from rifle shooting to squash, from chess to rugby. Inevitably this took place at the expense of academic achievement. End of term reports were usually heralded by the phrase 'could do better!' I enjoyed every moment of my public school days. I have no regrets, no opportunities missed. I look back with great pride on days well spent, days of achieving and days of hope and dreams for achievements to come.

I left school unwillingly, at an advanced age! My father managed to fiddle me various positions at both London and Oxford Universities, but neither would keep me. I lacked adequate academic qualification to take my place at either. My tutor at London decreed that I had an entrepreneurial business talent. How he knew this I do not know, but he has been proved right! All I knew at the time was that I was keen to get out and earn my living.

Ease of opportunity saw me join my father in his laundry business. I hated it. After the initial challenge that enthused fresh mind and, though I found that little could be done to improve the industry beyond the nationally accepted norm, a laundry provided a service to a customer, so long as the customer was prepared to accept the service that was on offer. To provide a quintessential customer service was then, and still is, beyond the ability of most of those who operate within the industry. I used the basis of the family company to diversify the group during the 1960's and 1970's. My father's critical eye continued to watch my entrepreneurial activities disapprovingly until his sudden unexpected death in 1979.

With too few years under the belt, and too little experience of life in its broader terms, I married my first wife at the age of 22. My hopes and plans for the future had always required immediate attention, so once I had reached what I considered to be a marriageable age, it had to be achieved. Neither of us realised that to have a truly successful and lasting marriage, understanding and acceptance of the other's needs in life are paramount if those two separate lives are to continue to live conjoined, albeit only at breakfast and dinner, at weekends and during periods of holiday. Nor had either of us appreciated, in our youthful innocence, that running one's own business would often make unreasonable demands on both parties. An inevitable slow erosion of communication and mutual ease was the forerunner of an inevitable matrimonial breakdown.

My partner for the last eighteen years (and my wife for the last three); we live, work and play together twenty four hours a day, every day of the year. That brings its own stresses and pressures on our individual persona, but we are incredibly lucky to be able to reap the benefits of such a way of life. It was thus Wendy who bore the brunt of that terrible pronouncement. I was too 'blacked out' to do more than absorb the impact of the whole. It was she who had suddenly to shoulder the burden of watching my mental decline, to try and propel us both forward into a future that seemed to be no future.

Thus our lives together intertwined still more strongly, and even now continues to do so. We had to come to terms with the prognosis. We had to throw off every aspect of our normal business life that we could, to enable us to spend what time we still had in doing everything in our power, not only to prolong our time together for as long as we could, but to fill it with days of memories to be held and treasured, not to waste a moment of the time we had left. We turned inward to each other to fight the doom, to plan for the enjoyment of each day and not waste it, while salvaging what small hope and encouragement we could from the mire of the prognosis.

In the eighteen years that we've been together we've been privileged to have done a great deal. We have travelled the world and founded a business on the other side of it! We have explored new business ventures, some of which have been financially successful, others financially disastrous! All have been mentally stimulating and enriching in one way or another. We still have to learn not to trust too much, as we have been nearly bankrupted on more than one occasion by ill-chosen colleagues and business partners. We dig deep into our mental reserves, retrench and come out again, such is the spirit of entrepreneurialism! To those who do not know us well, we appear well-breeched and financially secure. We remember the times when it has not always been so. We have always had the facility to fall back upon ourselves, and thus we are able together to take each day as it comes, plan it, use it and enjoy it. For if it is to be the first day of the last few days of the rest of a life, then to both of us it is important to use that day more comprehensively than we would ever before have appreciated.

Although those eighteen years were well spent in hard work, hard risk and hard achievement and nearly came to nought through the actions of others, life itself was seriously brought into perspective on that September day in 1995 which renders all else as 'nothing of importance'.

Without the strength and resolve of Wendy I might well have succumbed to the doom of my doctor; a lesson in team work. With the words of wisdom of Wendy, when that ache or pain seems to be heralding a fresh secondary cancer, I would find hope and the future that much less tangled. We lived and now continue to live one life, constantly in one another's company, constantly sharing most things, though my wife has hired a 'wife' to help with those things that I am too selfish to help with.

My contempt for the attitude of some within the health care system of Western medicine; the doom, the inevitable end, the continued crushing of the mildest confidence of my spirits encouraged me to debate with myself what was wrong. Hooked up to my Hickman line, with the tube contraption and its harness festooned around a series of bathside supports, I wallowed in a bath that eased the pain of my hip and pondered. I suddenly realised what it was that I believed to be wrong. Blind faith were the two words that had sprung to mind as I deliberated the past and beheld the doubt of the future.

With these two words summarising my thoughts, I decided that I must write that which is now my experience of my life and of life as it is beheld for others by others. I recognised that to infuse the majority of the practising medics within my circle of acquaintance with hope for myself, via a practice of self-help from a complementary medical source, was just not something that I could achieve. I reasoned that I was not alone in believing that there was a great core of medical belief in the infallibility of their judgement and practices. That the only way to penetrate that central core of resistance to a greater understanding was to try to enlighten others like me, that the prognosis of doom was not fundamental and that a change in that prognosis was possible.

Much more importantly, fit and healthy people should be made aware that there was more to fitness and health than their doctors meted out in cures for symptoms that manifested themselves from time to time. In other words, if I could reach the patient before he became ill, I just might be able to prevent him from becoming ill and would certainly, through him when ill, be able to reduce the impossible resistance in the Western medicine practitioners to the thought that they were fallible, and to the thought that there were sciences of complementary benefits to patients, which either as alternatives or when working alongside their faith, were able to cure ills.

It was with these thoughts in mind that I wrote Cancer - A Strange Gift; half in anger at the injustice I felt at having been denied, through ignorance, a remedy which might have helped me, and half in a desire to make others aware that they might help themselves by not being blind to the complementary help offered by practitioners of TCM, chiropractic and the like, who are not accepted by our own medicine world as people or science that can help.

Cancer - A Strange Gift is the précis of my life's medical ills in the past, with a more detailed account of a fight against cancer over the last five years, coupled with a fight against the unequivocal resistance of the Western medical profession to accept my ability and determination to help myself. No-one could have done more to encourage me in my fight than my TCM practitioner. The hope and determination he instilled in me is on offer to all if they can be made aware of its existence. It is this awareness that I seek to publicise, not only for those who are already in the throes of life threatening illness but also for the fit, for I am in no doubt through my own experience, that had I been made aware of the damage I was unwittingly doing to my own body during my adult years through diet and lack of understanding, there is a very strong chance that I would not have been struck by cancer of the bowel.

Such awareness is denied to most of us by our blind faith in Western medicine's ability to cure. This state of mind is exacerbated by Western medicine's blind faith in its own ability to cure and its unwillingness to accept the benefits that may accrue to its patients from complementary sciences. Even when it can cure no more, when the prognosis is one of doom, even when complementary medicine gives clear indication of its ability to delay that doom; even then, there are those Western practitioners whose only perception is one of incredulity and disbelief. What is even more damaging, and a sad reflection upon their blinkered state of mind, is the utter disinterest shown when orthodox medical prognosis is overturned. The expert who reads my six monthly scans is a prime case in point. He admits that he has never seen a tumour the size of mine remain unchanged for so long. He is amazed. He will say: "I don't know what you're doing, but it's obviously doing you good, so keep at it". When I respond, as I always do: "Would you be interested in hearing what TCM is doing for me?" his eyes glaze over, and he replies that there is an old adage which says if it makes you feel better to hang upside down from a tree by your toenails every day, then go to it .....

My secondary tumour is inoperable. That I have outlived the prophet of doom is due to the benefits of the radiotherapy and chemotherapy applied by Western medicine. I acknowledge that fact freely but I also believe that without TCM, my body would not have responded so positively and would certainly not have been able to support the additional dosages I was given.

I am a fatalist; I believe my tumour was meant. I wish that those who read my book are made more aware of the opportunities offered by complementary medicine for self-help from an early stage in life. Not just as an aid to cure an ill but as a preventative to becoming ill, so that they may have that which I was denied until it was nearly too late.

Hospitalised for 10 Days

"How did you know there was something wrong?"

"Because," I replied, "I noticed small amounts of blood in my stools".

"Why did you not do something at the time you noticed?"

"I did" was my answer, "I went to see my doctor."

I had indeed gone to see my doctor, and he had carried out tests which proved there was blood in the stools. It was his opinion that this probably resulted from my historical diverticulitis. Though I did not say it at the time to the nurse, that pronouncement, some 18 months before, had been accepted and I had rested since in peace.

Though she made no comment, the young trainee medical student who had been sitting on my bed obviously felt she had been talking to a fool. In her naivety and her total faith in what she was learning - that there was no room for fault or failure unless it lay at the patient's door. In this assumption she was probably correct, since most patients blindly follow the path directed by their doctor, in whom they have been brought up to have total faith. She left me to my own nervous reflections without further conversation.

Wendy and I remained in the admissions pre-operative ward of the John Radcliffe in Oxford for the prescribed period of twenty four hours before a major operation. I had never been seriously ill before in my life and certainly never had more than a hernia repaired under anaesthetic. In an effort to overcome the nerves I tried to think ahead to 24 hours hence, when we both hoped I would be back in the ward on the way to recovery.

My insurers, with whom I have been covered for twenty years or more and who, throughout my recent trials and tribulations, have behaved in the most dramatically helpful, sympathetic and reassuring way, were to pay for my private treatment in a National Health hospital. So when the evening came after that traumatic December day just ten days before Christmas, I was allowed a private room so that I could be alone with Wendy and undisturbed by the noises of the general ward, until she left me to my own devices for the remainder of the short night ahead. I was to be the first operation in the morning, and would consequently be woken very early.

The surgeon was charming, though I had only his reassuring smile from which to make this deduction. He talked so quietly that my middle- aged ears heard not at all what he said. I relied upon poor Wendy to relive each appointment after the event so that she could tell me exactly what had been said. I had met him briefly that first day in the John Radcliffe hospital and he had been the one who, a few short days earlier, had performed an endoscopy after which he pronounced that I had a bowel cancer. In his opinion it was removable and again, in his opinion, was not sufficiently advanced to have contaminated my body. A full recovery and a normal life expectancy, while in no way guaranteed, was hopefully a probability.

The forms that I had to sign that day were legion, as were the words of caution that I was told I had to be given. Most worrying, due to the location of the cancer, was the information that I might have to have a temporary colostomy. This clearly sat fearfully in the mind, for my first words to Wendy when I came round after the operation were "Have I got a bag?" "No!" was the answer I heard, which appears to have been the precursor to going back to sleep for some hours.

I had been told of the tubes that I would find inserted into my body after the operation. I had signed forms to say that I would not hold anyone responsible for anything that might go wrong! Each and every trainee who came to see me (and there seemed to be an inexhaustible supply) laboured some aspect of some problem which, however remote its chance of happening, seemed to be important to them to impart to my unwilling ears. Thus when the consultant saw me that evening he was bombarded by questions from my nervous mind, but the main one was 'the bag'. He reluctantly admitted the 'very unlikely' possibility.

A very young, very nubile, extremely pretty and perfectly turned out nurse came to measure me for this 'bag'. Where on my bulging middle aged torso could it best be sited? I had to stand and sit repeatedly while she pressed and probed to find the ultimate part of my anatomy where the tube should best penetrate the skin for the least discomfort. Eventually, with the flourish of a black indelible marker, an extraordinarily large cross marked the spot that she, in her wisdom, considered the focal point should be. Were the circumstances a little different, the experience could have been exciting. As it was, it merely served to increase my anxiety and focus my mind on things that I wished fervently were not about to happen but, which I knew if I wished to have any chance of living, had to take place.

The operation over, my gradual re-entry to post-operative life in a general ward started. The first hours of that day were passed in a semi-conscious state, with my wife at my side, and frequent visits from the nurses on the team to which I had been assigned. Each time one arrived I was told to press the button on my automatic dispenser, so that the pain killing drug was kept at optimum level in the body via a computerised control system and a tube into the back of my hand.

With each passing hour I became aware of more tubes attached to the body for drips in and drainage out. The milkman's basket lying at the bedside was introduced to me as the vehicle for carrying the drainage bottles. Sealed with a small reduction in atmospheric pressure, to allow a small but constant suction to exert itself to aid the draining system of the unwanted fluids in the base of the body adjacent to the operation, to the bladder and to the stomach. Soon I would learn how, with dexterity, to roll from my bed without becoming tangled with tubes; to pick up the milk crate and grasp the vertical steel tube which ran along the ground on castors; and (supported via a coat-hanger contraption above my head) the tubes and sacks filled with fluid which were feeding my body.

A careful chart of fluid-in and fluid-out was maintained at hourly intervals during those first few days. Far from being allowed to rest in bed, I was told to get up the day following the operation to walk around the ward, wheeling with one hand the 'food trolley' and, with the other, carrying the 'drain basket'!

The week before the operation, a day or two after diagnosis, my consultant gave me the option of being a private patient in a private hospital or attending an NHS hospital. Without thought, since I did not believe there to be a decision to make, I opted for a private hospital. The thought of not being able to be 'ill' in private was inconceivable from the start. To have one's own room and suffer in private was the only consideration as far as I was concerned. The consultant agreed but said that should there be any complications during the operation with which the private hospital would be unable to cope, then I would have to be 'brought round' and transferred. There was no reason to believe that there might be complications but the thought that if there were I might suddenly discover myself in an alien environment surrounded by all the people, equipment and horrors that the layman associates with operating theatres, in a powerless state, with an open wound, being moved to another location in a semi-conscious state was quite enough to make me consider the alternative and accept the advice proffered to go privately to the NHS establishment. I was assured that the consultant's 'team' of nurses there were used to him and to the idiosyncrasies of the patient and that they were brilliant.

I was in the next few days to realise quite the magnitude of correctness of that decision. The nurses were indeed superb. I couldn't eat, so the horror of the food that I saw being wheeled about was not of concern to me. Above all else, the presence and shared smiles of the other patients and the constant change and bustle of the ward helped enormously with my mental and physical security. There was no need to ring a bell for attention for there was an eye to catch all the time. The horror of wondering whether to ring a bell to summon help or advice, waiting and wondering whether to ring again because 30 seconds had passed and no-one had appeared was all in the imagination only and with happenings to watch, it must be assumed that the time might slip by faster.

During those three days after the operation while I was in the general ward, patients and nurses chatted to one another and gave one another support by merely being present. So how lucky I was to be 'ill' in the presence of others and be able to draw strength from the fact that we were all there together and the nursing teams were there to help as well.

Before the operation I had been visited by a physiotherapist, who had explained to me and indeed made me practise the method by which she would help me clear my lungs of anaesthetic after the operation. Deep breaths, held and then let go, several, one after the other, each one dislodging phlegm into the mouth. It is this event which is my first really clear memory after the operation, for the haze of the anaesthetic and sleep prevailed through the day of the operation and the night following.

On that first morning of total awareness, at an early hour, my physio arrived with a young white-coated girl in attendance. "This is X", she said: "She is on work experience and doing the rounds with me today. Would you mind if she saw your wound?" "Not at all", said I. As long as others looked and no-one expected me to even glance in the direction of the wound then that was great, for they would be able to assure me that I still had a lower half to my anatomy and presumably report should there be some evil happening. I was methodically stripped of bedclothes and nightshirt so that presumably the physiotherapist could check the status quo as well as show the work experience child the expertise of my consultant and his team.

My worst fears were realised. There was something horribly wrong with what had supposedly been an entirely successful operation. The colour on the little girl's face faded as though her blood had quite suddenly drained. She sank to the floor in a dead faint. Rapidly the area filled with nurses and my panic was suppressed even before it had started. All that had happened was the girl had passed out. Either she had never been exposed to the nether regions of the male before (which is improbable in today's age!) or merely the bruised and stitched scar some foot long had been too much. Anyway, the panic was over and I was told to sit up, having first pressed my pain killing dispenser button. I didn't believe it would be possible to move that much. I had been constantly aware over the preceding hours of the need to move only an arm, or preferably merely a finger and then only if the need was irrefutably defined and necessary. Such movement had of course to be very slow indeed in case pain resulted or more importantly, though lower in my list of priorities, a tube might become kinked, bent, dislodged or in some way have its vital job curtailed. The most important of the tubes seemed to me to be the one which ran from tummy, through throat, down nose and across the bed to disappear into the milk crate hidden from view on the floor beside my bed.

John Cook

There was no mistaking the determination of the physio. "Sit up" she said. So gingerly I sat up, all the time going through in my mind, how in the hell I was going to breathe deeply or indeed spit out anything that was in the lungs while a tube lurked in the throat and nose. What anyway was the point? I was breathing perfectly and couldn't feel phlegm in the chest. However I did as I was told. I felt no pain as I moved, no pain as I took a deep breath, no pain when the breath was held, no pain when the long held breath was exhaled and miraculously no problem with the phlegm which really did come up into the mouth. What a clever system and they really did know what was good for me! The second series of deep breathing was less successful and the phlegm went back down the throat into the tummy, whereupon it was 'whizzed' up the tube, past the throat, down the nose and ended up presumably in the bottle in the basket. 'Liquid out' recorded later as the bottle level was checked. All clever stuff. No sooner had the physio gone than the nurse assigned to me arrived, together with dear Wendy who had missed the first act of the drama but was about to witness the next, that of her hypochondriac husband being told to get out of bed. "You do realise that I only had my operation yesterday, don't you? I should not be expected to move too much and certainly not get out of bed so soon". My comments were greeted with mirth and determination for my nurse would see that I did get up.

Very gingerly and very carefully I eased myself off the bed, having pressed my 'pain button' long, hard and often before I tensed the first muscle of the little finger. Luckily I did not learn until later that the computerised 'pain button' would only let me have a measured dose, so that all that frenzied button pushing made me feel better but in fact achieved nothing at all! All worked perfectly. I was a little shaky on the pins but the tubes seemed to sort themselves out and there was astonishingly little pain from 'the wound'. My bed was remade and after a few halting steps I was allowed back in to relax and take stock of the fact that the worst was over and each hour should bring improvement, particularly and generally.

The routine of the day unfurled and, apart from deep breathing and a few faltering steps in the vicinity of the bed, the hours passed uneventfully. The ward was full of those newly arrived from the theatre, all or most having been operated on the same day as myself. The bustle never really stopped. The nursing shifts changed and darkness fell outside, but late into the night my doze was interrupted by my next door neighbour, who decided that it was time to go home! Complete with his set of tubes, his basket and his drips he got out of bed and started to head for the door. Nurses came from all directions as he protested that it was his right to discharge himself and discharge himself he would. Great commotion, great swearing. I learned a word or two! The pantomime prevailed for the rest of the night, for despite sedation the patient still wished to leave and no amount of bullying, cajoling or reasoning from the nurses could make the chap stay in bed. In hindsight amusing, at the time amusing to begin with, but when light dawned and a night of no sleep had passed, then irritation and indeed anger were well ensconced in my mind, for I was clear in the concept that we all need sleep and rest to recover and some madman let loose in the ward at night apparently beyond control was more than a joke at the time. My regret at not being a private patient in my own room in a private hospital confirmed itself as the night wore on.

The young houseman arrived the next morning with his attendant acolytes - all presumably on the steep learning curve. He found in me a crotchety and very bad tempered patient who wanted the tube to the tummy removed so that he could breathe and swallow properly. "Absolutely not." The command of an educated voice who, perhaps in wisdom and knowledge but certainly in terms of authority, was not to be argued with. I decided after a degree of truculent language to go over his head and talk to the consultant who I knew to be coming later in the day. I had the utmost confidence and faith in the nurses and my consultant, but this white coated official reminded me too much of bombastic prefects at school, whose word and authority were irreproachable despite the dubious wisdom of their commands. The contents of my bottle had remained virtually unaltered since the operation and I wanted to be able to do my deep breathing to discharge the anaesthetic from my lungs without the hassle of the tube, which tended to make me swallow that which I brought up and certainly maintained an uncomfortable blockage of phlegm in the throat akin to the catarrh of a heavy cold. It is true that what was swallowed quickly returned to the milk crate via the tube, but that really seemed a painstaking way of removing phlegm from the lungs!

By the second day I had become quite adept at shuffling about on my regular exercise course from one end of the ward to the other. I swapped my square wheeled supply trolley for one with round wheels on well oiled axles, which I could push with great precision through the melee of people and obstacles that littered the otherwise broad and long passage of the ward. My milk crate swung easily from the other hand and the plethora of tubes all rested steadily during the perambulations of the day.

My consultant arrived and even before I could pose the question stated: "It is time for your tube to be removed". I was told without preamble to take a deep breath and, before I realised what he was doing, he had pulled the tube out in one long movement. No hurt, no discomfort and the tube gone. I really felt I was making a good recovery, a positive psychological step forward. I had already forfeited the pain killing tube since the vein in the back of my hand had rebelled at the intrusion of a needle and a constant drip through it, and I had requested that the doctor on duty did not try to find another. I would, I thought, rather have pain in the gut than have someone trying to find a suitable vein in which to insert a needle. I was right, there was little or no pain from the operation area and a tube less meant a bottle less swinging on the wheeled chariot. Now I had but two tubes left for drainage, one from the bladder and one from the area of the operation. Real progress was being made even after only two days. I was told that I might be allowed a few sips of water later in the day, if I was really good and if all continued according to plan, I could expect to return to a private room two days hence.

Sadly I did not see the houseman again that day to gloat over my success, that higher authority had rescued me from his arrogant dismissal of my appeal for the removal of the tube.

I was allowed my sip of water and was told that I had to consume an ever increasing amount of water on the hour each hour. Since the volume even after six hours could scarcely be expected to drown a flea, the ordeal was not great and anyway I had always been used to consuming great quantities of water, so I was looking forward to the point at which I could drink a pint in one go. No other foods of any description were allowed to pass my lips and I was still only taking on real 'sustenance' via my drip.

The day came when I was allowed to move myself to my own room at the end of the ward. I had a window to look out of and a lavatory to myself, though that had no significance in my life at that time, since I had not eaten anything solid for the better part of a week and had also had ten inches of bowel removed. Most importantly, I had a place to myself to make a mess and the quiet and peace to think about what had happened. How very fortunate I seemed to be, how brilliant the nursing staff, and above all how marvellous were the medicine men in whose care I and others place ourselves at all times, whether the ailment is small or large, life threatening or merely irritating. A total faith in their ability to cure, and if cure is not possible then, well, it's nobody's fault; least of all the fault of the doctors, physicians and surgeons, if they cannot cure the malaise of the patient. I, it seemed, was to be numbered among the lucky ones. The operation had been successful and the cancer had been removed, along with a certain amount of stern tube and, as far as was possible to tell, there was no reason to believe that was not the end of the matter. Though, of course, no guarantees could be made and no certainty was attached to my apparent luck.

All good food for thought and the peace of the room was the ideal environment in which to collect myself together and to begin to contemplate the future while, as each hour passed and with each walk in the ward, I felt better and steadier and stronger. I was actually now allowed out of the ward and to wander, with other patients also regaining their freedom, about the floor on which my ward was placed. While brought together haphazardly and ignominiously by our various medical problems, a sense of deep camaraderie arose between us which for me enhanced the feeling of absolute security, a feeling I would not have anticipated given the circumstances! This, I believe, resulted from the steady routine of the ward from reveille to last post and a knowledge that I believed I was being given the chance to start again despite, as I saw it, not having properly cared for my body in the past and, more significantly maybe, the feeling of being part of something much bigger; the orderliness of the general hospital organisation. It invoked the conditions of spirit last known at school where, despite all the enormity of the problems at the time the institution, and as part of that institution oneself, ground on with seldom if ever a backward glance. Real life in the outside world is not like that for those of us who live by our wits, for whom tomorrow is uncertain, today hopefully constructive and yesterday an experience to be remembered and noted for the future.

Lying in bed at night, with nurses looking in and, if finding me awake and if fortunate enough to have a lull in ward duties, staying for a chat, was bliss. I was gaining confidence in the knowledge that the remaining tubes would not 'fall out' so, apart from sleeping or dozing on my back, I was actually brave enough to turn on my side and snooze while looking out over the city of Oxford from the heights of the sixth floor of the hospital. All seemed well until I moved without checking a drain tube. Immediately there was a slight tension on my tummy where it entered, followed by a great sigh as air travelled from I knew not where to the same destination! I pushed my little call button - the first time ever! Almost instantaneously there was the sound of many rushing feet and at least four nurses rushed into the room to attend to the emergency. I'd pushed the wrong button. I didn't feel as though I was dying, I had no great pain, all I wanted was attention and in my panic the wrong button had come to hand. I was mildly admonished but soon forgiven as Ann, who was in charge of me, was left behind to disconnect the tube and remove the bottle, it being felt that it was no longer necessary.

Having long since lost my feeding tube, the pain killing tube also having gone I was now left with one only from my bladder. Since I was now drinking water by the gallon I was constantly changing the drainage vessel and that also seemed pointless. However, it was to remain in for another day and it did at least provide me with the incentive to 'take exercise' by walking to and from the kitchen, where I emptied the container and recorded the liquid amount on the 'out' chart.

In spite of no intake of real food (nil by mouth still being the order of the day) I didn't seem to have lost weight and I didn't feel too hungry. The stomach was anyway full of water! But I was now seven days post operation and being told that, provided I had no temperature and continued to mend, I would be out before ten days had lapsed since that traumatic day when I had arrived early on the pre-operation day full of foreboding, worry and the multitudinous and varied forms of anxiety attached to hypochondria as can only be suffered by the male!

The day before leaving I was allowed to start eating a very little almost pre-digested food. I would not like to have stayed since food, even that not of a pre-digested nature, didn't actually appeal greatly, let alone motivate the saliva ducts!

I was to be home by Christmas; Wendy could stop her daily trips to sit with me in boring isolation in a tiny room on the sixth floor. My final tube was removed, the hole was sewn up and I could get dressed to go, the waistband of my trousers held together by an elastic band so as not to put pressure

John Cook

on the wound. Taking leave of my nurses and thanking practically everybody I could see for anything that came to mind, I escaped to the big outside world to convalesce and look forward to renewed life with expectation.

The Beginning of a Lucky Event

So ended a phase or saga in my life that had climaxed in the previous ten days. This event was directly linked to the fact that Wendy and I had spent some time with a widow who had nursed her husband through to a gruesome end from bowel cancer. He was just 43 when he died. A saga which had started a lifetime before, or so it seemed, as year after year my abdominal pains were attributed either to ulcers, a spastic colon or diverticulitis, but never ever connected by inference, suggestion or word from any doctor to the possible occurrence of cancer of the bowel. This despite my mother and grandmother dying of cancer, albeit at an old age, and my constantly inferred anxiety that I too might suffer from it at some stage.

It is to this widow, who had nursed her husband through to death from bowel cancer diagnosed too late, that l owe whatever extra span of life I may be privileged to enjoy. She came over from New Zealand for a few weeks in the summer of 1993 with her second husband, and Wendy and I undertook to drive her around Europe to show her some of the sights we believed Kiwis should see. Prior to her arrival in late June, I had not been feeling well, but there was nothing really to report in the way of symptoms other than a very erratic bowel, lethargy and an occasional feeling of sickness. My doctor felt that it was nothing more than the diverticulitis and colon spasm that was the diagnosis and ailment of the moment. I got on with life and set about planning our European journey. I had been plagued with aches and pains long since and they did not greatly affect my life, unless they were really excruciatingly painful, which did from time to time occur.

I specifically remember one evening in France, when we were sitting having dinner and Mary looked at me and said "Are you all right?" "Absolutely", said I. "No problem. Why do you ask?" "Because your face suddenly lost all its colour and became very grey". "I've no idea why that should be." I said. "I feel absolutely fine, thank you".

This sort of conversation was to repeat itself several times over the next weeks, but unbeknown to me Mary had also talked at length to Wendy about her husband's illness and the delays in diagnosis that he had experienced. As Mary explained, his symptoms appeared to mirror mine. And so it was that when we returned to the UK in September Wendy, again unbeknown to me, insisted that our GP arrange an endoscopy to check out the bowel and make sure that the diagnosis of colonic spasms and diverticulitis was in fact correct, that there was nothing more sinister lurking somewhere.

I readily agreed to the examination. I had always had total faith in my doctor, with whom I'd been at prep school and who had been my doctor for 25 years, since he took over the practice from his father. Down the ages I had always kept him informed of every problem and symptom. He had then prescribed the pill or prescription which had always cured the symptom. The colon spasm had a white pill, if the pain became more persistent he prescribed a yellow pill and if a temperature occurred I took a special antibiotic. All symptoms always reported and always eventually responded to the aid. Diagnosis as far as I was concerned had to be right and so I reported, consumed and appeared to mend, and thus contrived to have continuing unerring total faith in my good friend's ability to know what was wrong. Or, as I see it now, to accept that he had the remedy for the symptom. In my complete blind faith I followed his opinion, his diagnosis and his 'remedy' at all times.

A date was made for me to go into the private hospital to be examined by a consultant whom my doctor said was the best in town. No urgency was attached and a date was made for the end of October, some six weeks ahead. Nearer the time the date clashed with a race in which one of our horses was running, and since no horse runs unless we're present I sought to change the date of the examination. "Was there an urgency or could it be changed?" "Absolutely no urgency", they confirmed, "purely a routine precaution". So a second date was made at the end of November.

I attended the nursing home and met with the consultant, who spoke so quietly but had a lovely smile! I duly put myself into the hands of the nurses and under his care.

I didn't have a general anaesthetic but rather an injection of something to merely make me relaxed, so when the endoscope commenced recording on the screen I was, in a dozy way, able to watch. First there was this very inflamed and bloody patch and the last I remember was the 'swallowing up' of what appeared to be a black tadpole. Consciousness then left me and I remember no more until I began to 'come to' back in my room with Wendy by my side. So it was, in November 1993, that I heard through the mists of semi-anaesthetised brain the simple but curdling word 'cancer'. My consultant had just performed a colonoscopy; I was back in my room at the Acland and he was talking to Wendy while I grappled to fully appreciate what they discussed.

What I remember vividly was the horror of the diagnosis, mitigated only slightly by the consultant's words: "You are a young man, fit and otherwise healthy." He went on to explain that, as far as could be seen, the cancer was lodged on the wall of the bowel but appeared at this stage to be operable. He added that while there was no guarantee, he believed that the disease had been caught at an early enough stage for him to consider that life expectancy was not unduly threatened. But I was to have an immediate operation for the removal of the length of bowel containing the tumour.

Since the private hospital couldn't cope with 'operatic' drama and since my humorous consultant wished to make it clear that if there were problems during surgery I would have to be brought round and transported to the John Radcliffe mid-operation, as already stated, I opted to 'go private' within the National Health system at the John Radcliffe. The team was superb, the operation a success and within three weeks of hearing that horrid word I was back at home in time for Christmas having undergone what was said to be successful surgery, and having made what was said to be exceptional and dramatic post operative recovery.

Within four months, my caring GP and long standing friend considered me fit enough for a little diversion, albeit under medical surveillance. So we drove south through France in convoy with him and his wife, and spent a week in the sun at our French retreat. He and his wife then returned to the UK while Wendy and I spent a further ten days picking up the threads of the French business we had left the previous September. Little did we know then that we were only to make one more trip south, in the autumn of that year, before my further symptoms were to prevent us returning for an indefinite period.

During the ensuing year, I attended my consultant regularly for updates on the outcome of the operation. I also reported every lump and bump I could find to my GP. The prognosis was good. The consultant believed that the cancer had been eradicated and that, while I could scarcely come to terms with my good luck, I should as far as such predictions go, be mended. Certainly I subsequently met many people who have had the same operation as long past as twenty years, so I slowly became confident that I need perhaps not worry over energetically and that a normal life expectancy might after all be available!

By the end of 1994, a year after the operation, I was feeling fully restored and doing all those things that I had been used to doing, albeit with a degree of caution since, from being exceedingly fit, I had put on weight and maybe exaggerated my incapacities.

I've become a great fatalist and it is not unreasonable to associate the timing of the arrival of the widow and her message to Wendy as a life saver, though maybe the delay in the examination due to a horse race might perhaps be seen to be tempting providence. Nothing is sure in life, but it seems certainly reasonable with the added benefit of hindsight to predict that, without the widow's arrival and Wendy's prompting our doctor to further action, an examination would not in fact have taken place when it did and the cancer would certainly have been more advanced, perhaps even to a point of definitive no return.

What a chance event in my life and what a strangely lucky sequence of events that had started some years before which all contrived to bring the widow's message in time to give hope.

It is only recently that I have given thought to the negativity of medical opinion, medical action and medical diagnosis, for at the time of the operation I was still blinded by my faith in one man's diagnostic ability, one man's ability to prescribe a drug to offset a symptom and one system of medicine which in this case culminated in surgery to cure an evil, if evil may be used to describe illness. My doctor arranged for an examination and that examination was succeeded by an operation. In this instance the cause of recent malaise had not only been diagnosed but also treated and maybe cured. All good for the infallibility of European or Western modern scientific medicine and the faith in it placed by all those who live in the Western world, and maybe all who live outside modern medical systems but who look in to see perfect health care in operation.

Broader History of Ailments

From the very earliest age I can remember that whatever the malaise, or indeed accident, the saviour was the doctor. If the pain persisted, or if the cut was deep, always the doctor was summoned or I was taken to see him. He was a revered person who not always inflicted pain through a needle, but always seemed to be able to diagnose what was wrong and prescribe the pill or mixture that inevitably made me feel better. Not necessarily immediately, but always within a short time, the symptoms were declining and psychology did the rest. The moment the symptom started to abate I would forget about the cause, and when next asked how I felt I had of course forgotten about how I had felt before seeing the doctor. I do not believe I am an exception to the rule. We are all brought up to seek help in the ultimate stage of distress from the doctor. His subsequent diagnosis and prescription would inevitably appear infallible, since the symptom usually disappeared and probably didn't reoccur very soon, if at all.

Like most children, I recognised the importance of the doctor and his hold upon one's psychological approach to life, while I progressed through the normal children's diseases of chickenpox, measles and the rest.

Illness became something that I shunned and often didn't report because it might interfere with something that I wanted to do. This maybe strange outlook originated I believe from having pneumonia at the age of eight. I used to spend my days, when not modelling or fishing or making things, bicycling about in our village, where several members of the family lived. I would take 'elevenses' with an aunt, use the freedom given me by my bicycle to return home for lunch, and then maybe take tea with another aunt. In between times stabilising itchy feet by some more static employment of time!

My ninth birthday would be my last at home for many years, for it fell in July in the middle of the academic summer term, and for the next infinite number of years I would thus always be away at school. My parents had yielded to a small boy's pressure. I was to have a large, grand birthday party in the garden at home. Many friends had been asked, and my father had somehow managed to hire a helter skelter and other funfair items for our entertainment. I was a thoroughly spoilt child, effectively an only child since my sister was twelve years older. I lived and dreamed of the coming party, not just as the highlight of my life to date, but to keep me from brooding on the traumas ahead. Only a few more weeks before I was to be sent away to school for what at that age felt like a life sentence.

It may have been a day, it may have been two days, I do not recall precisely but it was certainly very close to the occasion of that great party that I suddenly began to feel unwell and quickly felt worse and worse. I told my mother, the doctor was summoned and I was declared to have pneumonia. I remember weeping buckets of tears at the cancellation of that party. I do not remember how long I was confined to my bed but I do remember that I was very ill and I suspect that it was several weeks before I was allowed up.

All too soon I began my first term at prep school, and discovered a further terrible truth about having been ill. I was, together with a poor unfortunate boy who suffered from asthma, singled out from the other 60 or so boys. My recent bout of pneumonia precluded me from playing games. I was conspicuously different. When others played games I was taken for a walk. When others rushed about outside during play times, enjoying all the sillinesses with which small boys let off steam, I was carefully wrapped up by the matron in layers of clothing, and allowed to watch from the sidelines.

I've no doubt this was all necessary for my long term good, but I had to endure these indignities for the whole of my first year, and I rather believe that it was this attack of pneumonia and its resultant personal anguish that in later years made me seek medical help only as a last resort.

Of course I could only put measles off for a short period, since I felt so awful that a declaration to this effect had eventually to be made, and off to bed I would go, forfeiting whatever it was that was important at the time - usually some sporting event! But flu and colds and aches and pains could be lived through. A good game of rugger followed by a hot shower usually prevented the onset of a cold, though of course the epidemic flu virus put me to bed along with the others.

As a games playing person I was pretty fit for most of the time while growing up, through participating in the various teams and events in which one represented school and county. So the doctor only really played a part when deciding whether or not I was fit enough to do something particularly strenuous or for the odd inoculation. Always in the back of my mind as the years passed, I had it firmly emblazoned that if something truly awful took place the doctor would prescribe a remedy to cure the ailment.

At an early stage in my university career I remember developing fairly severe abdominal pains. My doctor at the time prescribed rest and said that provided I put myself on a low roughage diet the beginnings of the ulcer he felt sure were evidenced by the pain would go away. The pains did go away, but for some years I was troubled by them, and occasionally took time away from either lectures or later work when they were too bad. They

John Cook

always lasted a few days and then went; their coming and their going didn't seem to bear any relation at all to my diet.

My doctor retired and his son, my prep school mate, took over the practice. The new mind took a new look and I was told that I had colitis and a spastic colon. The remedy was a little white pill called Colofac that was predominantly peppermint, was not addictive, could do no damage and could be taken as often as I liked when a pain was persistent. The pain was a movable feast, sometimes low down, in which case Colofac was the remedy; sometimes higher up on the left hand side when if the pain persisted for a day or two I would take a yellow pill, a Motipress. With the aid of the two 'cures' my symptoms would inevitably go away and I would have weeks or sometimes months free of pain. I never contemplated the cause of the pain. I had faith in my doctor's diagnosis. I accepted that it was the result of colitis or whatever, the cure for which was a white or yellow pill. The cause of colitis was never mentioned. If a conclusion was ever contemplated, which it wasn't seriously, I suppose I believed that it was something inherent in the design of my body, rather like a hand maybe! The outcome was always "What a clever doctor I have! He understands what is wrong with my body and can be reliably expected to produce a cure".

As well as having spasmodic pains in the gut I, along with millions of others, suffered from a 'bad back'. In my late twenties I found that a local osteopath or physiotherapist (call him what you will, but a man referred to by my sister as her 'back

40

man') to whom I went, to see if he could sort out a lower back problem, could indeed enable me to play the games I wanted to; to do those things that I wished to do without creating a problem with the back. I attended him weekly for several months and he sorted out for me what he described as a twisted pelvis. He also was categorised in my mind as a miracle man, for he had sorted that which on occasions was a very debilitating pain. His 'cure' enabled me to continue to live the active life I desired without pain.

So armed with a now not twisted pelvis and yellow pills and white pills I continued to work and play hard, doing all those things that I wished to do, from running my business, to gardening and from sitting in a car to playing many varied and different games.

Then with the advent of my second wife I acquired a new miracle science, a chiropractor. I first went to see him as a result of a minor car accident. Over about ten years of fairly regular visits to the chiropractor it became evident that he could not only provide effective treatment for my back problems, but interestingly he was also able to alleviate the pain which had always been associated with the diagnosed spastic colon. Right at the beginning he had X-rayed my spine and pinpointed damage to the fourth lumbar vertebra, which I had presumably had for many years. It was certainly not as a result of the very minor shake up that we had received in the motor car accident. It was, he implied, the result of a fairly serious injury years before that had caused a fracture that had healed badly, leaving a weak area in the spine. This vertebra is apparently connected directly via the nervous system to the colon.

Gradually I was able to depend upon manipulation or chiropractic formula instead of swallowing pills. My pill intake was drastically reduced, and the periods between pains often ran for months and not weeks, as had been the case for the previous fifteen years or so. I was still very actively playing games and generally enjoying a hard working and hard playing life. But the pains, while far less frequent, were becoming on occasions beyond pills. Relief came instantaneously from a session with the chiropractor. My doctor was unable to find a clinical explanation for the benefit derived from the chiropractic technique, but he did organise for me a barium examination of the colon, a matter which I found rather off-putting in principle but quite fascinating in fact. The entire colon from bottom up is filled with barium and then scanned onto a screen for the experts to examine. It was angled so that I was also able to see what my insides looked like! The medical diagnosis at the time; nothing sinister present, just severe diverticulitis. The appearance of my gut, they said, resembled that of an eighty year old: I was only forty five. My medical knowledge is sufficiently limited that despite various explanations I accepted this latest diagnosis as an extension of colitis. If the symptoms worsened dramatically, I was told, it was merely a matter of a simple operation to remove a few inches of the worst affected area. All was well, or as well as might be expected of a gut of such an apparent age and, with the advent of chiropractic which supplemented pills, I was able to do most things most times, except occasionally when the pain was very intense.

And so the next few years slipped by. They brought the depression of the late eighties and early nineties and with the depression came worries the like of which I had never before experienced. Like so many others, I was deserted by business friends and colleagues as the economic climate changed. Like so many others, I was on my own. When you run your own business there is nowhere else to pass the buck, it stops right here! At least I had the good fortune to have a wife with whom I worked to share the burden, but there were few to turn to for help. The most conspicuous of deserters was our banker who suddenly changed his spots, economic and financial ruin seemed to lurk around every corner. Despite the bank's fickleness we weathered the storm created by government and financial institutions, we were lucky. We stayed in business: just.

During all those worrying months my pains were noticeably absent but I did notice a certain amount of blood being passed in the stools. "Diverticulitis," my doctor said. "You mustn't forget that you've got diverticulitis and that is undoubtedly responsible for the blood." He sent blood samples for analysis on several occasions and seemed not to be perturbed. I still had my utter faith in him, despite the unexplained benefit from chiropractic, and so thought no more about the causes of the continuing but not incessant blood.

John Cook

We went abroad and got down to work exploring other avenues more exciting and worthwhile, while government, bankers and England, not to mention our poor, hard hit employees, got to grips with the changing situation.

It was as a direct result of our foreign business activities that we found ourselves entertaining in France the New Zealand widow who conveyed to Wendy her anxiety over my oft bad colour and pains. It was Wendy who in the autumn of 1993 persuaded my doctor that I should have another internal examination to set minds at rest.

It was this examination delayed by a horse race that showed that I had a cancer in the bowel wall, and it was presumably this cancer that had been producing blood for a year. I assume it is possible that the cancer resulted from the deteriorating gut of an 80 year old despite my being only fifty two, aggravated perhaps by the stress and worry of the period. Is there a link between the fourth vertebra, the colon and the gradual deterioration culminating in a tumour? Could it have been foreseen that this sequence might have been anticipated? I am no doctor of medicine, merely a patient, but from what I now know it seems very probable that had the colitis been 'treated' to cure the problem, rather than to cure the symptom, then my life expectancy might not have suffered. The threat of death is always present when crossing the road but one knows the odds on that and can take precautions. The threat of death prevails from all sorts of illness, but if the patient is enabled, through knowledge, to treat the cause rather than the symptom, then it must be obvious that the removal of the cause of the problem is likely to be more beneficial than the elimination of the symptom only.

John Cook

Misconceived Peace Between
Operations

Christmas 1993. Recuperation, post operation, started. I was told to do not a lot, but I been told that I'd made an exceptional post operative recovery and I saw no great reason to deny myself anything in particular. I was severely reprimanded for chopping wood too soon and my bowel was definitely not to be relied upon. I got used to the term 'follow through'. A fart might part company totally normally and then, when least expected, it might create a problem. A 'nappy' was definitely the order of the day - and night. But gradually the system became more reliable despite the missing ten inches. I came to regard what I call 'the stern tube' as more and more predictable and by April, four months after the operation, we embarked upon a trip to France for an extended break and to take up the reins of that which we'd been working on in

France, where the economy at that stage was, for numerous reasons, significantly healthier than England. It was also a much better business climate within which to work, not least because of a more desirable banking system.

I returned every three months to see my surgeon. I assumed that as well as checking on his handiwork, of which he was not unreasonably proud, he was also checking around the area to ensure that all was well. He expressed himself well content with the healing process, though never produced a satisfactory explanation as to what happened to the titanium staples he had used to join both ends of the stern tube! At each appointment we would enquire, from a position of total ignorance, whether it would be a good idea to take a course of chemotherapy to zap any wandering cancer cells that might be present. He was at pains to reassure us that he saw no reason to suppose that the operation had not successfully removed all offending parts.

We had faith. All seemed well, and in October of that year, nine months after the operation, was told that we could reduce the appointments to six monthly intervals. The nappies had been discarded and there seemed no lasting ill of the experience. Life was steadily returning to normal and with each month that passed, I was led to understand that there was an increasing belief that the cancer had been totally cured. I was not told what symptoms to look for in the event of a recurrence of the disease. I was told no more than that, provided my surgeon could have a proper check every six months, if no adverse condition of the bowel in the vicinity of the operation had occurred at the end of five years, I would be passed fully fit. I could see no other reason for him wishing to examine my bowel each time I visited. It is true that he had a prod in my stomach and where I now know the liver hides itself, but the reason behind these prods was never explained.

January 1995. It was with excitement that we accepted a commission to go to the Bahamas for a month to 'trouble shoot' the completion of a friend's newly built house so that it should be in good order for the letting season which started in February. They were concerned that things were not proceeding as smoothly as they should, and were unable to get out there themselves.

I consulted my GP who said that I could indeed go off for a month. I also knew that I was seeing my consultant shortly after returning. So it seemed that I might gently re-enter the world of international travelling to attend the businesses that we own or run as far afield as New Zealand, which had perforce been deprived of our presence and help, and greatly neglected during my convalescence. It seemed a God-sent opportunity to take to the air again and seek out some winter sun.

The narrative that follows highlights, with the obvious benefits of hindsight, the odd irregularities of the system which started to manifest themselves during the month we stayed on Harbour Island, and which were eventually diagnosed as a secondary cancer of significant proportions. Initially, they merely proved an intermittently painful irritant.

Hindsight can be many things. I now know that the night passed in the airport hotel in Miami (by virtue of the time differential, a wonderfully long night which provided a much needed break for recuperation after the flight from Heathrow), was to be the last night I was to sleep through without having to get up for at least one pee. Until then I'd always slept soundly through the night and had hardly ever had to get up, certainly no more than once.

The following morning, refreshed and excited by the day ahead, we boarded a small plane to Eleuthera, and from there took a taxi down to the ferry for the short trip to Harbour Island. We met the appointed taxi driver, who cheerily deposited us at the house, promising to return with the two bicycles he deemed essential for our local transportation.

We duly settled in, checking out the things we'd been sent to check out, and trying to get done those things that had not been done. We discovered that the Bahamian builder is no more competent than builders in any other part of the world that we have encountered. The lavatory basins were not screwed to the floor and wobbled about alarmingly, the draw wires for the telephone cable pipes were missing, and the usual problems of sloppiness were evident all over the house.

John Cook

Almost immediately upon our arrival I was beset with the need to urinate frequently at night. At first the demand was maybe three or four times a night, but it steadily increased until prior to the eventual diagnosis, I was having to urinate every half an hour. Constipation became the next problem - one which I had never had in my life before. During the day my lavatorial habits did not appear to change significantly, although I do remember having suddenly to relieve myself over the gunwale of a hire boat!

It is perhaps worth reiterating that for the previous thirty years - since leaving school almost - I had been diagnosed as having an ulcer, troublesome bowels, diverticular disease, etc, would report to my doctor on a fairly regular basis to replenish stocks of Motipress and Colofac and when abroad would travel with an antibiotic specially related to bowel infection, a state that had applied for 15 years or more. The symptoms were pains in the abdomen and a constant diarrhoea, so constipation was a new experience. I attached no special significance to either, merely taking them in the stride and getting on with the job in hand - chasing the local tradesmen to get the building contracts finalised and a house fully available for the commencement of the tourist season.

Another problem that manifested itself almost immediately we arrived was a stiffness and soreness in the left hip. I was first conscious of it when we wandered down the garden and waded into the wonderful tranquil sea for our inaugural swim at the end of our first day. My steady breast

50

stroke evidenced clear discomfort in the left hip, but I was inclined to attribute it to long flights in cramped conditions and assumed it would wear off with regular exercise. When it did not, and if anything began to deteriorate, I assumed that something was awry in my lower back and resolved to see my chiropractor on our return to the UK.

Our food intake was mostly lobster! We consumed one a day for 28 days, since we both love the crustacean we were in our element. We devoured wonderful fish and consumed copious quantities of wines and fresh fruit juices. The fact that I needed to get up in the middle of every night was an irritant, but didn't either concern or register in my mind as something to worry about. In the morning I would wake up with a slight headache, it wouldn't last long and was a hangover, albeit very mild, or so I thought. The wine was chasing the lobsters down very well! Both headaches and nocturnal peeing became the norm, as did an increasing reliance on magnifying glasses to read, even during bright daylight hours. I assumed the problem to have been caused by the wine and dismissed the problem for what I believed it to be - gluttony! A necessary requirement for a strong drink after spending too long chasing someone else's contractors, who invariably obtained by fair means or foul the upper hand and left one feeling hopelessly inadequate to do the job that we'd agreed to do.

But we were achieving and we were enjoying ourselves. Such minor physical inconveniences were of little concern since they didn't create problems of moment. To get up in the middle of the night and to spend time enjoying the nocturnal beauty of the place was no hardship. The lap of the waves at the bottom of the garden, the moon and clear stars unaffected by the neon glow of an English night, the calls of the animals and the rustle of leaves were all pleasurably different and enjoyed greatly. It was good to be alive and awake and living at a time when normally I would have been sound asleep. The reason for being awakened each night didn't impinge on an otherwise peaceful mind.

Wendy and I reluctantly returned home at the end of the month to report that the lavatories were properly assembled and working, the telephone had finally been connected and several other matters of import had been relegated to the finished department as opposed to pending.

Upon our return to England we set about planning a trip to see our business partners in New Zealand, since it now appeared that I was able to resume a normal active business life. Having been self-employed all my life, I knew the import of getting back into the swing of things not only for mental stimulation, but also to ensure that those things which should be done were in fact being done. I had already delegated, thank goodness, to trusty and loyal people most, if not all routine jobs long before my illness. Thus my time during my illness and convalescence had been very much my own; but that does not mean to say that one can get along indefinitely doing nothing and leaving all to others.

Within a few days of arriving back in England the headaches began to intensify and last longer, but a normal pain killer seemed to eliminate them. Then, as the days passed the headaches began to become a worry and the nightly peeing became more frequent.

We had been back in the UK three weeks and it was only six or seven weeks since the symptoms had started. Each week it seemed they had got worse. I never had a clear spell of more than perhaps three days and the headaches gradually took on problematical proportions. I couldn't blame bad wine or hangovers or too much too rich food - I was in England again!

So I went to see my doctor. He took my blood pressure and found that it recorded 180 over 130. Never having had to relate to such things as blood pressure before, the figures meant nothing to me but they did to him!! He took samples of blood and urine and gave me strong pain killing pills together with a drug to reduce the blood pressure. Hypertension was his diagnosis, something that can happen in middle age for reasons as yet unknown to the medical fraternity and affects over 10% of the population over the age of fifty. Something that happens to the middle-aged regardless of having just had a wonderful Caribbean winter holiday with no pressures?

Reduction of the dangerous level of blood pressure would take place with pills. Such pills would be needed for the rest of life to maintain the blood pressure at an acceptable level. Hypertension has no cure, it just has to be controlled by drugs. He prescribed Bendrofluazide and Enalapril , the quantities of which he gradually increased until, over the weeks, the pressure came down to 150 over 100 or so from where it was reluctant to move, and where my doctor said it was temporarily acceptable.

I had my eyes tested and my brain scanned, and while the oculist said that there was visible damage caused by the blood pressure which would repair with time, the brain scan was totally negative. For some months my eyesight had been deteriorating to the point where I wore 1.5 magnifying glasses if I wanted to read. I certainly couldn't read a newspaper without them, and even with the benefit of magnifying glasses, reading small print was out of the question.

Despite the use of pain killers and blood pressure drugs, the headaches continued to intensify and become more prolonged. The daily intake of the drugs to control the blood pressure was increased and the doctor reported that the urine sample and blood sample were normal. He went on to tell me that what he'd believed might be present, cancer of the prostate and/or of a remote gland, were definitely not. This was the first time I knew that they might have been, he hadn't told me before.

Over the weeks the pill intake increased dramatically, both painkillers and beta blockers. The headaches gradually became less intense and more spasmodic, until by March they were a thing of the past. But the bladder remained a constant nuisance. During the day it seldom allowed me more than an hour between relieving its pressure, and by night it was a routine half hourly requirement. At this stage I believed and said that the activities had become psychosomatic. I was suffering from irritable bowel syndrome now as well as malfunction, but nothing that really prevented life going on more or less normally.

In the middle of March, around the time of the Cheltenham Festival (a date I remember well since our good doctor and his wife came with us to watch our horse run), on the Thursday of the meeting my 'cravings' stopped, as did my appetite. As early as January I had craved for something but couldn't find the answer. I tried savoury, I tried sweet. I tried fish, meat, vegetables, fruit - everything and anything different that I could lay my hands on, but nothing answered the call of that craving. Even in the Bahamas, all those lovely fresh fruit and fish and vegetables helped not at all. Now the problem went away of its own accord, as did, to an extent my appetite, which up to then had always been good. I was known in the family as 'The Hoover', for I would always finish off other people's left- overs. That stopped abruptly.

I attended my consultant in March for my six monthly check-up and despite high blood pressure and poor lavatorial habits, he seemed happy enough with my progress and didn't want to see me for another six months. I left feeling that the cancer may indeed have been removed.

But the magnifying glasses that I'd taken to using and the nightly water passing showed no improvement. Indeed the regularity of peeing was on the increase and the eyesight was continuing to deteriorate. By May I had reached the point, despite all manner of urinary and water retention drugs, where I had very little warning of the need to urinate and often had to just stop the car get out and relieve the pressure.

We have always travelled many miles every year for business purposes. Until this point in our lives we had devised a very satisfactory way of covering whichever country we were in. I would drive and Wendy would navigate. Thus we would be reasonably sure of arriving at our destination in good order and good humour, the system worked well! But now, with the increasing pressure on the bladder, we reversed the roles - though my navigational skills were not of great assistance since my eyesight had deteriorated. So Wendy drove, and I sat in the passenger seat with an empty bottle. This meant that to stop was no longer necessary, I was able to pee 'on the move'! When we did stop, my car door would open and to the amazement of people on the pavement I would empty my bottle into the gutter! Mild amusement was had by Wendy and myself for we were still lulled into the belief that the problem would be diagnosed and cured.

During the period, my doctor tried various pills and potions to try to cure the urinary problems, and repeatedly tested for cancer of the prostate, and of some small gland adjacent to the kidneys which can produce high blood pressure. All proved negative which was a relief, since I was convinced I had a return of my cancer.

Our holiday letting business towards which we'd been working in France looked as though at long last, despite the strength of the French franc, it might just be going to produce a good season. We were behind ourselves with execution of plans because of my previous illness but ahead enough to look forward to something happening. So accompanied by my doctor and his wife, we set out in May for the south of France in two cars. My bottle accompanied me, ensuring that our progress south was not hampered by the need to stop every half hour. My blood pressure was going to be checked upon arrival and I was going to be told whether or not I could exercise on a bicycle. I had taken no exercise at all since swimming in the Bahamas several months before.

Another symptom now developed. Before Christmas, five months earlier for we were still only in May, I had been doing some furniture carrying, quite heavy furniture, and quite difficult 'lifts'. I had a sharp and painful pain in my left hip that was debilitating for a little but it passed. When swimming in the Bahamas it had reoccurred, but by dint of continuing to swim the pain seemed to ease and before we'd returned, it had gone. A pulled muscle seemed the most probable cause. But now the pain returned and as the weeks passed it intensified. I started taking painkillers again though they had little effect.

John Cook

The journey down, the stay in France and the return trip to England for a few days passed uneventfully, except for the fact that at the end of a day's drive I had a pain in the hip. This soon dispersed after leaving the driving seat, and I thought little of it other than it had been brought on by sitting in one position for an extended period. It felt rather like a sciatic nerve problem with which I was familiar, since for years I had suffered from back problems brought about by a youth too full of rugger and other good gamely pursuits.

Wendy and I again returned to France in our trusty Espace at the end of May, to pursue our business enterprise and replace business neglect with attention. At the end of the first day's drive my hip was painful again, and I decreed that I would see a chiropractor when we got to our French base - we had used him before and knew him well. My headaches had gone and, while I was up every half hour at night, the system seemed to have adjusted so that I did not feel too greatly the lack of sleep which resulted.

During the weeks that followed my hip, despite chiropractic intervention, got gradually more and more uncomfortable until it produced a limp and a pain, which further interrupted my already disturbed nights. So we returned prematurely to England at the end of June to report back to my doctor. By this time the leg was showing every symptom of a trapped sciatic nerve with pain in different regions of the leg from hip to ankle, and no real reprieve after chiropractic manipulation.

I'd had a scan of my head and torso and now my doctor arranged for me to have an X-ray of the pelvis and lower torso to see what was causing the problem with the hip. Apart from vestiges of arthritis consistent with my age, nothing untoward could be seen. I was, by now, increasingly of the belief that I was riddled with cancer, but I was assured as the tests were carried out, the scans completed and X-rays performed that this was not the case. This could not dissuade me from my fear.

Meanwhile I was still getting up every half hour during the night to relieve the bladder pressure and that wasn't as easy as it sounds. If I had the urge to spend a penny nothing would happen. I would have to stand by the lavatory dangling the useless tube I'd always called a penis until the urge to urinate had gone! Then I could pee - not much, but enough to alleviate the pressure and enable me to go back to bed for a thirty minute doze. The whole operation took maybe ten minutes by which time I was again wide awake. These interrupted and sleepless nights didn't seem to make me very tired by day, so I imagine the body compensated for the reduced sleep pattern. By day there was less problem for I would relieve myself regularly, without waiting for the need - the 'tube' seemed to be able to cope with this!

I spent much time with my chiropractor. He couldn't find out why my hip hurt so much but he did discover that movement in the leg was decreasing. I was certainly now walking with a limp, I couldn't stand or sit for more than ten minutes or so at a time and consequently found

John Cook

travelling increasingly difficult. I couldn't drive since my left leg was painful when asked to depress the clutch, and couldn't anyway sit for long in the seat of a car.

Heading Towards Secondary Tumour

By the middle of July 1995 I was unable to stand, sit or lie down for more than half an hour without the need to move to relieve the pain in the leg. I was spending an ever increasing amount of my daylight hours lying on the floor on my stomach, the only position I could find where the pain was relatively bearable. This was my only reprieve. I was frequently to be found in this position in the garden in the sun (thank God for a lovely summer in England!) and in the office. In fact I continued to work face down.

I could run away no more, I was captive to my pain and immobility. I frequently fell over as the muscles in my left leg wasted. I took to using a stick for support. I continued to work, but my progress about a factory was now so slow that I couldn't catch errant staff! The clump of the stick gave my presence away so that I couldn't even rely upon the element of surprise!

Looking back now, I really don't know how I managed to do anything at all with the continual encumbrance of such a level of pain. Even to survive each day took every ounce of my determination and will to live. There were moments - not many, but enough - when I would have been glad of oblivion.

My doctor now presented a physiotherapist to treat the malfunctioning hip. He put me face down on a moving bed, turned on the power and the ends of the bed then went up and down, flexing the back and simultaneously the hip. I did not enjoy the sensation but I did get a little relief from the treatment. This took place three times a week. Each time I left his consulting rooms, I would hobble up and down the road with Wendy, testing for relief and looking for positive improvement before getting back into the car to return home. The benefits of the rigorous exercise lasted for a matter of hours only before the pain and immobility returned. The whole scenario made the headaches and previous problems fade into far distant and minimal proportions.

Still my GP persevered. More tests were done, more blood and samples taken. After each one I was told that another possible cancer site had been eliminated, although at the time I was unaware that this next test was yet another test for cancer in another part of the body.

His next action was to refer me to a neurologist to investigate the lower spine, in the belief that it was the old lower back injury that was at the root of the problem. Another consulting room, another expert. He was charming and thorough; I was checked out by him in detail even to the 'finger up the bum' which now seemed to be the norm in any examination. "I'll not be using my scalpel on you" he said. "But you must have an MRI scan of your lower spine as soon as I can arrange it". There was no mention of cancer, no suggestion that the scan was for any purposes other than identifying the lower back problem for which I had been referred to him.

He was as good as his word. Within three days I was attending the MRI unit at the John Radcliffe. Wendy and I were confident that this scan would expose the old injury as the root of the evil. Once identified, it could readily be dealt with, we fondly imagined, even though it might limit future mobility in some form or another. I think that was as far as our contemplation went. We were happy in our belief that the neurologist had finally correctly identified the problem. Again, no thought of cancer entered our minds. Why should it? No mention or even inference had ever been put forward.

I duly went through the procedure of medical claustrophobia within the MRI machine. Being of considerable width across the shoulders, I was unable to slide into the constriction of the scanning tube with my hands by my sides. I therefore went in feet first, arms above the head, with a wife hanging onto the outlying hands for comfort!

The scan completed, Wendy and I emerged into the small waiting area. I was told to get dressed and that the doctor in charge would see me immediately. He duly arrived, a long, lanky man I had never seen before in my life. He looked around, asked me to identify myself and when Wendy and I came forward he drew together three chairs, motioned us to sit, called for silence in the room and in none too sotto voce tones said: "I am afraid you have a recurrence of your disease."

There was a very long pause while we assimilated what he was saying, and while the other occupants presumably wondered what it was all about. Finally, the penny dropped, "Do you mean cancer?" I asked.

"Yes" was his reply. "You've a tumour the size of a golf ball on the left side of your pelvis. It is eating into the bone, pressing on your bladder and destroying your hip joint. But don't worry, there are things we can do!"

Thus we were made aware, in the baldest of terms by a man neither of us had ever seen before that, for which I had gone into the machine, namely a scan of the lower spine, had produced a far more serious and dramatic revelation. The delivery was both brash and unsympathetic. This man, this technician if you like (for as the 'reader' of the pictures emanating from the machine that is precisely what he is) then proceeded to enlarge upon his first momentous pronouncement. There was a tumour growing on the soft tissue of the floor of the pelvis, he reiterated, but not to worry, he affirmed yet again, there were things that could be done.

He left us then. He made no mention of the neurologist who had sent me, and with whom we have had no professional contact since, though I did write to thank him for his actions, since without his input who knows how long it might have taken others to follow the correct diagnostic course of action? He did not say that he would report to my GP. He did not offer any advice or any suggestions. He merely got up and walked away to carry on with his job.

We were numb I think. I remember that we stood up and looked around and then went to leave in a rather bemused fashion. Our need to get to the fresh air was arrested mid-flow by a child behind a desk, who wanted a form completed and signed to ensure that my insurers would pay. We were bemused, we were in a kind of mental limbo. I do not know what was going through Wendy's mind, I only know that my worst fears were crystallising and taking real shape. It was the end of August 1995, I was fifty-four, I was in a bad shape physically and now none too good mentally!

The shock was horrendous, the more so since I'd been enduring so many symptoms for nigh on six months. They'd been getting worse day on day and week on week and yet all that time I was being told that cancer was not the problem. Yet all that time a simple MRI scan would have given the answer months earlier. The tumour might not indeed have been the size of a golf ball if I had been scanned at an earlier stage. I subsequently discovered that when it was finally identified, it was 8cm across and about the same height - a real championship sized golf ball! A cricket ball would have been a closer analogy!

During the months which followed my bowel operation, I would seize all positive aspects that might point to my surgeon being correct. I might indeed have been one of the lucky ones who had been diagnosed in time and have had the primary tumour cut out in time. Then I would think, "Why should I be so lucky? It will probably get me". I would begin to get depressed because there was so much still that I wanted to do with my life - I felt I'd hardly really started, all that had gone before was the beginning so to speak. Mentally I have always been a fatalist; what was destined 'would be' and all that 'had been' was for some purpose in one's life. Thinking this was custom, and meant that life's purpose was maybe guided by life's experiences provided you saw the experience in that light. I'd come to believe that the experience of having had cancer, and maybe having been given a new lease on life as a result of modern science and surgery to expurgate that cancer, was in some way to guide me for the future. It had most certainly awakened me to the present, made me more aware of every day and that which was heralded by the day, my focus was now on enjoying every aspect that each new day provided.

Now, in the few short moments it had taken to listen to the flat interpretation of the MRI result, the hopes seemed to fade, the panic started. We drove back from Oxford, although we remember little of it. We went to see my doctor. He had, of course, neither seen the scan nor had time to think coherently. He had, however, talked to the man who had conveyed the news to us, the man upon whose interpretation we all now rested.

The good news, if you could call it that, was that we now knew the cause of the hip pain and what was creating the bladder problems, but what could not be related to the cancer was the blood pressure. There was, my doctor stated, no clinical reason for any relationship between the two. Though this statement was later to be contradicted by another doctor at another examination.

The other good news, according to my doctor, was that the tumour could be removed by radiotherapy and finally killed by a course of chemotherapy, so all was not lost. My spirits and Wendy's hopes were raised and panic was replaced by a euphoric belief that even now, despite a secondary cancer growth of significant proportions, science and modern medicine could still with luck save my life and, it was said, restore me to normal. The radiotherapy would harden the damaged hip joint, the chemotherapy and reduction in the size of the tumour would enable normal functional restoration to the bladder. There was no talk of blood pressure for this was, with daily pills, under control and anyway this was something different. It was caused by hypertension, a problem affecting many people in middle age and caused by forces unknown.

John Cook

From having been seriously knocked about by the first news, the mind reacted to the positive news by climbing to euphoric levels. It was going to be all right, modern medicine would deal with the problem. We telephoned our best friends and said "Please join us for dinner, we're celebrating a reprieve .... ." In hindsight this was maybe the most important, yet apparently unrelated, decision we'd ever taken.

Over dinner, the problem having been thoroughly aired, Jane asked if I'd ever thought about Chinese medicine or herbal concoctions, or even going to see someone who practised such things. I hadn't. My non-clinical brain had been made aware of the world of complementary medicine only in terms of chiropractic, and my blind faith in things medicinal of Western origin, and my long standing faith in my doctor in particular, was only now being alerted to other options. It is too strong a word to use 'shattered' in relationship to the blind faith that I had, for I certainly still had that unquestioning faith. The science of chiropractic had merely awakened me to the knowledge that there can be - not alternative medicine, for this is not a correct interpretation - but a complementary scientific approach to many ailments. Without Western medicine and science I would, after all, not have had the diagnosis which ensured that I had my bowel operation 'in time'.

At that stage I did not have reason to consider that, if the cause of my earlier problems had been treated rather than the symptoms, then the need for surgery might never have arisen. Indeed I still do not know that this can be convincingly argued. The facts are that the symptoms were treated, the resultant progression to cancer, if progression is what you may call it, may well have been resultant upon not having the cause treated, but it was removed surgically by Western medicine. Now there is a secondary, which is definitely resultant from the primary which was treated and this secondary is, it seems, also able to be treated by modern Western medicine. Thus the hypothetical logic argued by some, that complementary medicine could have saved the trauma, that my ignorance of that and my dependence upon Western medicine and the blind faith I had in it actually resulted in my body becoming cancerous, was not and cannot be proven.

So when Jane mentioned her Chinese herbalist, my mind was very much open to the suggestion that I would like to see him to explore ways in which complementary medicine could help. Some years before it would most certainly not have been. I had no faith, let alone blind faith, in TCM for I'd not been brought up with it. Rather I had been brought up to believe that the doctor could cure all and there were many quacks around from whom one should keep well clear, for they practised a science which was neither understood nor safe.

Jane said she would ask him if he thought he could help me. The wheels were thus set in motion and thank God they were, for hindsight dictates that my medicine man, for that is what I call him, helped me immeasurably in the months to come. Events so often seem to occur for the best when viewed

John Cook

afterwards and that dinner certainly was no exception.

Within three days of the MRI scan, I reported to an oncologist recommended by my doctor after lengthy discussion regarding hospitals, their location, their efficiency in dealing with cancer and oncologists themselves.

We reported to the Churchill in Oxford, Wendy and I. We were led without words to an airless little room with windows of frosted glass that didn't open, a room filled with the paraphernalia of modern science as it relates to medicine. We sat there for some time. We made a pathetic attempt to keep our spirits up by making fun of the sign above the hot tap which said 'Caution! This water is hot'. We tried to open a window, any air or life that could be breathed into that dingy little room would have eased our depression. We tried and failed. Then we merely sat, deeply ensconced in our own thoughts, to await the arrival of the oncologist.

The consultation and examination, for the oncologist was another who wished to shove his fingers up the bum, lasted for maybe half an hour. Armed with the knowledge that my doctor had said I could be cured, I was not unreasonably apprehensive when after examination we started to talk. My apprehension grew as the conversation progressed and cures became out of the question. The tumour was inoperable due to its position on the pelvic floor. So what else was available? Radiotherapy and chemotherapy in some shape or form to be decided. My thoughts on simple curatives sank without trace under his replies, to be replaced by definite question marks relating to life itself.

I was probably foolish, but after his examination and during the discussion on what treatment I should have, I asked him what life span I might expect. "Ten years maybe?" "No. Not at all" was the bald reply. The answer took us both aback. After a brief silence while I cogitated the inference of what he had just said I asked: "Well maybe five then?" He hesitated, then again replied, baldly stating: "If you were to make five years I would expect you to be seriously ill by then. I am prepared to say that a year could be reasonably expected".

He went on to say that one of the prime benefits of his 'treatment' was that it would enable me to lead what life span was left to me as normally as possible. He inferred that it was his job to improve as best he may, the quality of that remaining time. In response to my query as to what I should and shouldn't do, could and couldn't eat, he responded that much play is made of the benefits of diet and 'fads' in these situations. In his opinion there was absolutely no point in guzzling carrot juice to the point of turning orange, it was not going to make a stitch of difference and so if I wanted to eat steak and chips then I should do so. In his opinion it would make no difference to treatment or disease to deprive myself of anything. Indeed, the only positive statement he made, if it can be read as a positive statement was "Many people talk of diets on these occasions. I wouldn't advise you to pay heed to them, eat what you will when you will and enjoy your food" ("for in a year you'll be dead anyway!" he didn't add). He went on to outline that I could expect a course of radiotherapy and chemotherapy to arrest the disease and he would work out quantities in due course and be in touch.

Thus it seemed that in the space of a few minutes, in a rather tawdry little back room in the Churchill Hospital, the opaque windows of which blotted out even the car park outside, life expectancy and hope had literally been removed.

I grasped at the straw of Bob Champion, the jockey who had been cured of cancer. "Don't relate to him. His was curable and yours is not," was his curt response. I didn't continue with the line of questioning for it was obvious that my life was to end soon. All that was on offer was that he would, with chemotherapy and radiotherapy, do what he could to obviate pain and current symptoms for as long as he could.

His clearly stated conclusion was that I would live for a year with luck but the prognosis was definitively finite, for no cures existed and if I lived for five years I would indeed be a very sick man. A year was the best.

Hope Lost & Regained and a New Friend for Life

I couldn't breathe; the windows wouldn't open. I couldn't see; the room was barren and clinical with nothing to look at. My hands broke into a sweat, beads of it dripped from my finger tips. I didn't faint but I thought I was going to. I was in a state of shock, probably the understatement of a lifetime! All I wanted to do was to get out, to breathe real air and find space for myself.

"No, you can't go yet" said the consultant as he left the room. Wendy and I sat on in stunned silence. He had gone to arrange for a chest X-ray. I hadn't had one, he assumed? He also needed to get blood tests carried out. "You will wait here for me". We waited. I in chilled terror, Wendy in disbelief and misery.

There was a looking glass in the room. There was nowhere else to look. The room was a cell. I looked at myself. I felt so awful, and what I saw brought no encouragement. The face that stared back was expressionless and without colour, drained to resemble a death mask. We waited and waited. We waited an age in the cell, nothing to distract me from reflecting upon these new constrictions imposed upon my life. Eventually a nurse appeared and directed us about the hospital for X-ray and blood tests. We sat about in yet more airless, dingy corners waiting for the various technicians. On the way out I asked each time: "Can you tell me what this shows?" grasping at the air for consolation, knowing that I would achieve no information from what they said to me, but unable to desist from asking. They said nothing. I knew they could say nothing but there was no encouragement, nothing to buoy up the spirits.

Tests completed, we returned to the arid room with the frosted windows to await the oncologist. We were still numb, still silent, still unable to absorb and comprehend the whole. When he finally reappeared, the oncologist said he would be in touch to tell me when to report and where to report to have a Hickman line put in to receive the chemotherapy. We were now free to leave.

We rushed from the hospital in a frenzy. We had to get away from the place, the room and of course the prognosis, but the latter couldn't be left behind so easily.

We faded away to our home and clung heavily to our closest friends without whose support we would not have survived. They, between them, ensured that we were never alone of an evening and always had something to do. In short, they were marvellous and gradually we began to come to terms with what had been said and to come out of the haze in fighting mood. But how to fight? What weapons could we employ? Was there anything out there that could actually help to prolong that life expectancy rather than merely make what was left less painful?

As the days passed and as the supportive company of our friends progressed on each individual meeting, so the sense of doom was lifted marginally, to be replaced by a sense of the present and a disregard for the future. Even in the company of those friends I could sit in silence with my thoughts, until eventually their continued conversation absorbed me. I knew that I couldn't just sit and think for a year - if that was all I had left to me it would be such a waste of that year. But it was a strange period of dawning realisation, in an odd way the dawn of a new life, every waking moment needed to be extended and captured in its every aspect to be remembered and savoured in detail.

My doctor was no help. When I appealed to him for more positive support than that which the oncologist had declined to proffer, he merely stated that he had asked the specialist 'not to be too hard' on me.

I thought about that statement a lot. I construed that he had produced hope in the first instance where there was none, and that he had deliberately withheld information from me material to my life and life expectancy. We had even celebrated over dinner his prognosis of a cure, which had been followed so firmly on its heels by the oncologist's dismal estimate of my life expectancy. To me, that was false information, falsely borne. For the first time in my life I looked upon him not as a friend but as an alien who maybe knew nothing and certainly was not to be trusted. If I had only months to live, it would not be to him that I would turn with my customary blind faith, for he had now abused that faith. I would have to turn to him for help, but of necessity not will. I would hear what he said but I would no longer believe, would rather seek confirmation or clarification elsewhere.

It was in this state of awareness, and with no hope in my heart, that I went first to see the Chinese medicine practitioner, who had reported through Jane that he would like to help and that he had made an emergency appointment for me to see him.

I reported to his clinic with Wendy. In our separately vulnerable states we were both ready to grasp at any straw that might produce hope. But what hope? Hope for today?. Hope for counselling?. Hope for a cure? Just hope for understanding, for a chance to talk, to empathise, for it was clear from the handout of mental torment produced by the knowing medical faculty, that there was nothing but the dietary enjoyment of food to be expected over the next months, while my body deteriorated gradually and life's end loomed closer.

We were ushered into a tiny room full of fragrance, into the company of a man whose smile, countenance and presence were all consuming. His father was Irish and his mother is Greek. He is as English as he can be, down to his Oxford degree, yet to me from that first moment when we met, he will always be 'my Chinaman'.

My Chinaman listened to all I said; to all Wendy said. He took my pulse, he looked at my tongue, he looked at my eyes and my skin. He asked questions relating to my medical history and he became agitated when I told him that I only had a short time to live, as this is what I'd been told. I told him I was to have radiotherapy but I didn't know when it would start, and that I should have chemotherapy via a Hickman line to be inserted into my chest to provide a continuous drip feed of the poison, but I didn't know when.

"That's good" he said. "That's the best way to have the drug and I can help your body gain the most benefit from both radiotherapy and chemotherapy by making the body work properly. You are going to get better by yourself, I can only help you to help yourself. You will fight the disease and you will fight the doctors who say you will die and you will prove them wrong. They had no right to say what they said for they do not know. There are many people who should have died from cancer whose lives were threatened and whose prognosis was maybe for only a few weeks or months of life expectancy. They're still around some twenty years and more on. There are those who die who should not have died. So do not think negatively, think positively and you will live, you will fight, Western medicine will help and I will help. We can conquer the problem together," he said. "You're young, you look well and I can work with modern science so that that science can be used to its maximum efficiency."

He had literally squeezed me in between appointments but still he was prepared to devote time to my case and above all to our minds, instilling in us both a feeling of purpose and hope rather than a feeling of waiting for the day of doom. He again checked pulse, eyes and tongue and asked what type of chemotherapy had been prescribed. I told the truth, I did not know. Several days had passed since I had seen the oncologist and I had heard nothing from him. So all I knew was that at some stage in the future, at a date yet to be determined, I was to have a Hickman line installed and a consequent continuous dose of medication twenty four hours a day, seven days a week for an indefinite period.

The fact that I knew so little other than that I had been prescribed a twelve month life span incensed my medicine man. "Send the oncologist a fax," he told me. "Ask for immediate clarification of what is happening, what will be happening and what might be expected to occur. Sharpen him up. Let him know that you mean business and, above all, get some action and stop allowing the system to procrastinate even for a day or two. Start, in other words, to fight. Fight for life, fight for what you want and, above all, let everyone know that you are there and expect the best. If you fail to receive the best, let them know that they will be called to answer for anything that may occur, as a result of anything they fail to do properly."

He then outlined his proposals for my treatment by TCM (Traditional Chinese Medicine). This was to include a regular supply of high dose Vitamins B, C and E, supplemented by Selenium and Psillium (plantain) capsules to regularise the bowel. Turning to diet, he insisted that I eat only white fowl and fish, as much oily fish as possible. I was to cut out all other meat, shellfish, smoked products, dairy foods and eggs. No animal fats of any description, but vegetable oil should be taken. Protein and carbohydrate were not to be taken at the same meal (the principle behind the Hay diet). The daily intake should incorporate plenty of fresh fruit and vegetables, together with cider vinegar. This would cut out the turmoil in the digestive system and result in greater efficiency, so that the body would have more energy to devote to combating the disease and the poisonous effects of the chemotherapy treatment. He then proceeded to write out his herbal medicine prescription which his receptionist made up while we waited. "This to be boiled up and taken twice a day. You will cure yourself of this problem" were his words as I left his house.

And so there it was, a ray of light, an instigated need to help myself, an urge to live, an idea that life was still to be lived, that it might be prolonged beyond the dismal estimates of modern science. I'd been there before, at the time of the operation and afterwards, but I'd not been there during the months of incessant pain and I'd certainly not been there since my consultation in that dreary little room at the Churchill.

What a contrast with this small but lived-in room, full of colour and life, and a man who encouraged me, who promised me that I could do so much to help myself. Who encouraged me to get on with just that, and not to wait for the wheels of modern medicine to grind slowly on. "Force the pace, keep on top of it, keep yourself moving forward", was his exhortation.

When I got home, I sat down and I contemplated that which I had just learned. The miracles of modern science could be complemented by the traditional cures of a medicinal approach founded upon thousands of years of knowledge which might bring answers. Certainly if I were to continue to follow the blind faith I'd hitherto had in Western medicine I was, I was told, doomed to a few short months. So nothing could be lost in a positive approach engendered by a science new to me and about which I knew nothing, but which would soon reveal itself in two surprising ways.

Firstly, though my Chinaman would comprehend Western medicine and its place in cures, the opposite was not true of the Western medicine man. He had a blind disregard for TCM and a blind faith in his own powers even when confronted with unexplainable changes in me which were contrary to his expectation. He would still not remotely attach any significance to my being treated by a complementary technique. Not an alternative technique, but one which worked with Western medicine and from which, as a patient, I was clearly gaining benefit. This must question the Western medical approach, for surely anything that brings relief to distress should be encouraged not scorned, nor flippantly dismissed on the 'if you think it helps you to swing from the trees by your toes, then by all means go on swinging' principle that I have had to listen to so often. Just a little interest, even if not meant, would go a long way to maintaining a patient's hope and his determination to fight.

I have subsequently heard that the same oncologist to whom I had been referred, recently refused to authorise an MRI scan for a patient whom he had diagnosed as having a limited life span. The patient, with advanced cancer of the liver, had refused the oncologist's proffered chemotherapy treatment. Instead he had chosen to follow a course of TCM and changed his lifestyle and dietary habits. Some months beyond the life span that the oncologist had allowed him, and feeling in much better health, he visited the oncologist again in order to ask him to arrange a scan to see what had happened to the cancer. The oncologist refused, claiming that the MRI scanner was a limited resource whose use should be restricted to those who like me, were following orthodox methods of treatment. How can a doctor, who is by definition caring of body, reconcile such refusal to care for the mind and spirit?

The second contrast came much later when I was suffering from acute radiation burns. The actual application of the different techniques for treating the radiotherapy burns is widely divergent. The Western approach involves steroid creams and drugs; the TCM approach is the use of aloe vera juice, both internally and externally. The former did not work, the latter did. The Western medicine man was not prepared to heed the result. While he acknowledged that the burns were not as severe and debilitating as he would have expected, and thus I was able to withstand more radiotherapy than he had originally envisaged, he was totally unable or unwilling to consider what might have caused such an improvement.

But the real difference in concept was that TCM was treating my whole body as one, balancing it, the better to enable it to deal with the ravages of modern life. And the mind works with the body in a total sense of 'complete' healing. TCM treats the causes, the root problems of a body's imbalance. As a result, the body's own efficiency can fight illness and prevent illness without recourse to drugs. Western medicine in many instances will treat merely the superficial symptoms of deeper causes.

I left that first appointment with my medicine man, the first encounter with an alien world, with hope. Mentally I had been brought up short; throwaway negativity and grab with all my strength positive thought. From that day on I was to follow a strict diet. I would eat three meals a day with nothing between and there would be at least four hours between each meal. I was placed on a hybrid of the Hay diet, which forbids the mixing of carbohydrate and protein in the same meal. I would eat a protein meal once a day and I would eat a carbohydrate meal once a day. I would eat fresh vegetables and fresh fruit and wherever possible not consume food containing preservatives. The die was cast, help yourself by doing something for yourself. The diet was a positive approach, and one which totally contradicted the oncologist's pose of 'eat how you like now because you'll die soon anyway'. Added to the basic principles of the Hay way of thinking, I was to eat only chicken and fish, vegetables and fruit. I was allowed no spirits to drink and no white wine but I could, with food, indulge in a little red wine and beer or cider and of course fruit juices and water were allowed. Absolutely no tea or coffee.

And so, while Wendy emptied her store cupboard and fridge and started to get to grips with a whole new principle of cooking the right meals, I began to learn about herbal teas. Mint water, verbena, lime flower and a host of others. No tannin and no caffeine, but a new age of imbibing hot drinks which were both pleasant to the palate and digestively helpful. Not habit forming and now consumed by us both in prodigious quantities, though it must be said that Wendy has yet to wean herself from her morning pot of freshly brewed coffee! In France, you may ask for 'une infusion' anywhere anytime and receive an appropriate pot without demur. In England, even in the most 'advanced' gastronomic establishments, a request for a herbal tea usually elicits the response "Is Earl

Grey OK?" and if you then suggest they merely pour boiling water over a few fresh mint leaves (which you know they've got to hand because your sorbet's just been decorated with them), they look at you as if you should be certified!

I was to take vitamins B, C and E in massive doses on slow release pills and was to take, twice daily, my personal decoction of specially prepared Chinese herbs. Most importantly I was told that all would commence as from then. From that day on I was to start to fight a battle that would not be easy, that would have its trauma but would be worth it when I proved the doctors and the prognosis wrong.

Since nothing had happened and nothing had been heard from the oncologist since that awful day in the Churchill, it was my task to begin first with Western medicine by attacking the system that had said, "You've a year to live" and then wasted nearly a twentieth of that limited life span, before even beginning to prepare me to receive the treatment! I was to send faxes to the oncologist and to the consultant informing them that we expected the best treatment available and that that treatment was to be forthcoming without further delay. Since I still saw the surgeon who had performed the first operation, I was to call his secretary and try to get him to attach my Hickman line, so that the oncologist would realise that if he didn't perform to the best of his ability someone else would, and he might be attacked for negligence. The whole scenario was effected to get me back in the driving seat which, with the medicine man behind me, would enable me to get up and get on rather than sit around and await that which I'd been told was inevitable: death - quite soon.

Upon leaving our new found friend boosted in morale, under no illusions that I'd been granted life but definitively under the spell of a man and a system which promised hope where there had been no hope, Wendy and I rushed to the shops to buy the vitamins prescribed and to undertake the first elementary stages of the new shopping scenario. We'd always eaten plenty of vegetables but intake was to be increased and purity questioned. I had no thought that the enemy I'd engaged was going to be a pushover. I'd no idea whether or not I'd win and pull through, but for the first time I'd got hope and for the first time in my life I'd been given a way of helping myself, rather than just sitting around to await the automatic 'healing' of medical science's latest idea or drug. Also I had the concept that I was embarking upon a journey often undertaken by countless people in the Eastern world many times before. Presumably some were successful, or the TCM we know today would not have lasted for thousands of years, and would not be taught to the outside world and maybe, most important, would not be learned by people of my medicine man's ability unless he and they were convinced that it could help, if not cure.

The instructions we had been given for 'brewing' the herbs involved two lots of boiling up and then mixing the two decoctions. As luck would have it, it was a colleague of my Chinaman, having a day away from his London practice, who volunteered to put together the bags of herbs we would require. He strongly advised that we invest in a 'slow cooker', one of those earthenware pots with an element underneath, and use that to brew up overnight. That way, he said, you will not endure the powerful smells that emanate during the process. We followed his sound advice that evening and the next morning after breakfast I sampled my first Chinese 'brew'. I wasn't at all sure what to expect but what I discovered was that which I expected least, indeed had never contemplated.

Way back in the Bahamas I'd yearned for that elusive taste. I'd tried sweet, tried sour, tried acid, tried everything in a search for that which my body craved. Not finding the solution to my body's request the need had gradually subsided and had eventually been extinguished, along with a diminution in my appetite, culminating that day in March six months earlier. So I had forgotten about it, other more important things seemed to take a place in my mind, more painful things and more worrying things. Now with that first taste of my Chinese 'brew' all those yearnings were re-awakened in my system. That first gulp having re-awakened the need also satisfied the desire, a quite extraordinary occurrence but one which is quite true in every respect. That brew and each successive brew has satisfied a need, has satisfied a desire and has been not just enjoyable to drink but downright satisfying as though it created its own demand and provided me with something hitherto missing from my body. Few believe me when I show them my decoction, and tell them that I really enjoy it, but again it is a fact. I wake sometimes in the early night in a panic lest I'd forgotten to take it before going to bed, but my dear wife doesn't allow that omission and I return to sleep remembering that I had in fact taken my nocturnal dose. It may be said that I'm addicted to it, but I'm sure it's not addictive it is just that, unlike medicine, my body wants and needs it and continues to do so, and it helps the body to be whole in a way that no drug can. That whole body, that healthy and efficient body which incorporates also the mind, is now more resistant to infection and objects to intrusion. So without scientific proof, I believe that it is now doing battle on its own account with the alien cancerous body that it wishes to reject.

The Fight Begins

I wrote my fax message to the oncologist, having checked with my doctor that he was indeed considered to be the best man for the job, and that the supposed treatment was correct. I also asked him to make arrangements for me to go to the Acland immediately to have my Hickman line put in so that, when action did stir, I was ready to receive whatever that action might produce. I- we - felt stronger and in charge once again of our destiny. It was true that we didn't know what the future had in store but we never did - who does? What we did know, was that we were going to fight and hopefully win a battle against not only the horror of the disease, the word and its connotations, but also the doomsday negativity and insensitivity of those who looked only on the bleak side.

So, I had been taking my 'brew' for a week before having my Hickman line installed and a few days of the Hickman line before the chemotherapy started, so TCM was playing a role within my body even before the first drops of poison entered. I am not going to say that I felt better, for I did not. I was still deeply worried; the poking and prodding had produced appalling bowel problems and there were times when I sat for what seemed like hours evacuating blood and bile in quantity. I was told not to worry - it was just the symptom of the tumour's proximity to the bowel, but I found it hard not to worry, in light of what had gone before and the assurances that I'd already received from those in whom I'd had blind faith. Certainly prior to the start of chemotherapy the bowel had settled a little, probably as a result of not being prodded, but possibly because of the beginnings of harmony within the body resulting from the balancing being effected by TCM. It comforted me to think so.

I was to be under the same surgeon's knife again, but this time the operation was small. The installation of the Hickman line which went, as I understood it, from heart to an outside position for connecting to my continuous chemotherapy line, and it was to be done privately in the Acland in Oxford. I would be an in-patient and my insurer would cover my expenses. This raised in my mind a worry over the future costs, for I was only insured for being in hospital, I was not covered for being a day patient. The radiotherapy treatment would be taken as an out-patient and the same would apply to chemotherapy, it looked as though I would be uninsured.

This was of concern since I knew not what the cost might be, other than I was sure it would not be cheap. Since I had already embarked upon the treatment as a private patient, I couldn't now convert to the NHS, and the NHS wouldn't provide the new technology of continuous drip-feed chemotherapy - said by all to be a preferable way of having the drug administered. My insurers had been asked to adjudicate upon what they would and wouldn't pay for, so I could do nothing but await their decision. They would be perfectly within their rights to refuse to pay for all treatment since it was all to be outpatient treatment.

The immediate concern was the anaesthetist. I was taking many blood pressure pills, without which no doubt the pressure would ascend to the trauma heights of before. He gave it some thought and finally decided to give me some kind of light local anaesthetic which wouldn't render me totally unconscious. Even though I could feel nothing, I was aware of my surroundings and could hear in a vague way. I'm told that I carried on a conversation throughout! I know not of what I talked and I've no idea if my idle chatter was returned! Upon coming round I was subjected to excruciating pain from my hip. I had not been able to lie flat on my back for months, only flat on my tummy, so I became the first patient the nurses could remember, to be transported from operating theatre to ward lying on my front. I had the first step to treatment being administered behind me, I felt on the way to actually trying to combat my disease, and I felt I had had a hand in it, since it was I who had gone direct to the surgeon rather than waiting for him to come to me. I was indeed taking charge of my own destiny.

By this time, in mid September 1995, I could not walk without a stick, and even then progress was slow and limited. I could manage maybe 20 yards before needing to stop and rest. I could sit in certain positions only, and then it was a matter of trial and error to get comfortable. Even when comfortable, the duration of sitting was seldom more than fifteen minutes before pain forced me to move. I could kneel on a chair until the knees became sore, which was of slightly greater duration! I could lie on my tummy for maybe half an hour at a time and the same duration of time passed while I lay on my good side - mostly at night. I could stand a little but the muscles in the leg were so wasted the leg was only half the circumference in the thigh of the good leg, so that standing for more than a few minutes was tiring and painful. I really had to keep moving which was just as well since the bladder needed attending to every half hour, morning, noon and night. I was at the time philosophical. I grinned and I bore it, for there was nothing else to do, but writing about it now while it is still fresh in the mind and, I can now sit for as long as I like without pain of any kind, makes me wonder how I coped at all.

Some days later I attended the Churchill with my plastic Hickman line neatly folded and plugged off protruding from my chest. I was to be connected to the first batch of the drug. I was briefed by a young nurse as to some of the possible side effects of the chemotherapy drugs. From mouth ulcers to cracked skin, from loss of appetite to nausea, hair loss, nail loss and the rest, the list seemed endless. Little of what she said stuck in the mind at the time. I suspect little of it was meant to, according to law, etiquette, patients' charter or whatever, I had to be told and she told me.

I was then connected to an exceedingly neat tube of chemotherapy (5FU) packed under pressure in an inner tube visible to the eye which would 'pump' 5mls per hour into the system. No pumps, no motors, no wires, no complications. Just a tube of plastic to protect the tube of rubber connected via a yard of polythene tube to my Hickman line.

The oncologist arrived at this point and showed me how this sophisticated infusion system was supposed to be attached to me. He produced a nylon bag into which the tube fitted snugly. He then produced one exceedingly small gold safety pin. To which part of my attire would I like to attach it? Wendy and I pondered the question. The tube was about eight inches long and over an inch in diameter. I had each tube for a week, was I supposed to remain in the same shirt for a week for fear of creating a malfunction through the weak link of attachment? And how could one tuck such an unwieldy object out of sight?

Finally, we gingerly attached the little pin inside the shirt, where the waistband of the trousers would ensure that the tube couldn't fall out. It was done - with a little help from us the 'system' had provided me with the wherewithal to continue the fight against the disease that my Chinese medicine man had said could be beaten, and with which he had already started to help me.

Wendy and I departed home where we settled down to try and invent a system of portage for the tube which might be rather more reliable, safe and easy to use and less conspicuous than the bag and one small pin supplied.

We experimented with all sorts of 'slings' but finally, with painstaking efforts by Wendy, and after trying many different designs, we arrived at the current 'holster' made from stretchy crepe bandage which holds the tube snugly under the arm beneath the shirt. We were encouraged by the district nurse, whose job it was to swap tubes and flush out the line, to patent and market it. Such is the perceived need for this kind of item in the scenario of advancing applications of medical science. There are seemingly all sorts of chemicals dispensed by similar tubes for different illnesses. We haven't done so, so I imagine that the little gold safety pin still holds sway!

The following week we returned to the hospital to collect more tubes for the district nurse to attach to me. A digression in the practice of the treatment, conceived by my doctor as being easier than having to commute weekly to the Churchill, along the appalling traffic congested roads which habitually surround Oxford. We could collect three tubes at a time, and store them in the surgery refrigerator. Upon getting them back to the surgery they were found not only to be of a different shape and duration of medicinal output, but also malfunctioning in that they were leaking chemical. Neither fact improved my ongoing peace of mind. Were we to spend each week modifying the 'holster' to fit a different tube? If the tubes were faulty what faith might I have in anything that was supposed to be applied (at great expense, for I am a private patient) to save my life or at least prolong it?

I settled down to write a condemning fax to the oncologist but before it could be sent further catastrophe occurred. My tube had to be changed, and the tubes we had just collected were all faulty. A call to the pharmacy at the Churchill confirmed that they would replace them, so poor Wendy had to battle her way to Oxford and back yet again, in the thick of Friday evening traffic, to collect the replacements. She did just that, bringing back three tubes in their red 'dangerous chemical' polythene bags. Exhausted, she delivered them and me to the surgery. When the outer container was opened the tubes were of the original design. Relief spread through those assembled - my doctor, the district nurse, Wendy and I.

Then the bombshell - the first tube was clearly leaking, as was the second. The third mercifully was not, so at least the mission could be accomplished and a new tube fitted, even if future stocks were useless and would have to be replaced yet again. My fax was altered, became stronger and threatening. If this was what you got when you paid for it, pity those who had to rely upon the NHS. What confidence might one expect to acquire in the treatment, when there was total disarray not only of application but of the treatment itself?

I had two weeks of chemotherapy before I started radiotherapy. I stuck relentlessly to my diet, my vitamins and my Chinese 'brew'. An ulcer so small as to be hardly noticed appeared in my mouth for a day or two and then vanished. I thought myself into nausea but never left anything on my plate. I thought myself into all sorts of imaginary problems but they never materialised.

I became aware of perhaps a little less pain in the hip, though this was probably due to the increased intake of morphine that I had now been prescribed. My blood count, which was supposed to fall, actually increased. I'd been told that my immune system would be at such a low level that I would be susceptible to any bug or virus going about. I caught nothing. In fact after the combined treatment had been working together for only a week or so some symptoms appeared already to be improving. I could go to sleep for an hour at night instead of the customary half hour.

My next concern was simple logistics. If I was to get to Oxford every day for radiotherapy how best to go about it. Why the problem? Simply, the road network around Oxford is so poorly designed that traffic all day every day is spasmodically chaotic. To make an appointment at a fixed time daily would result in acute anxiety every journey, lest one was held up. That was before you got into Oxford itself. No-one who doesn't have to visit Oxford should ever go there. The City Council have devised a traffic system which creates havoc on a regular basis; furthermore they have enrolled a whole regiment of obnoxious officials who fine one for parking in the City in any but authorised locations, which are inevitably always full. They ask that you use their 'Park and Ride' system if you wish to get into the City centre. If you are unwise enough to follow their suggestion and you do indeed park in their car parks outside the City and take a bus as requested, you stand a reasonable chance of finding that your vehicle has been stolen or damaged while you have left it, the risk being the inverse on its value!

As if a prayer were answered, a dear friend offered us the use of the flat over one of her offices in Oxford for the duration of the treatment. It was a gesture of enormous generosity which we gratefully accepted, used, enjoyed and very much appreciated. I'd never lived in a city before with all that it entails, from proximity of shops and buses to take one to them, to the bustle to be watched from the window, for it was autumn and I couldn't walk far. Even then, the first night we spent there our car was broken into because it was parked in Oxford's crime infested centre and we got a parking ticket, because I couldn't walk far enough to get from the flat to the nearest parking. Wendy would bring the car nearer to make it possible for me to get to it. While she was assisting my slow passage from flat to street, one sly warden found time to slap a penalty ticket under the wiper! There is no doubt that Oxford has become, as a result of City Council policy, the unabated crime wave and the absurd traffic congestion both in and out, a city for all to avoid.

Since I was not 'permanently' disabled I did not qualify for a disabled sticker for my car!! The law seemed to overlook the fact that I could be disabled until death, which apparently is an altogether different situation to one who is permanently disabled! Ridiculous, but the absence of parking dispensation created many problems even within the hospital grounds where I was supposed to be being treated! So much for petty officials and officialdom.

I had attended the Churchill. I was now attached to my tube of chemotherapy. Painless, uneventful and unexciting but I really felt now that I was arming myself, tooling up, for the battle ahead. I was on a diet, taking vitamins, taking a decoction and now taking chemotherapy. I had a deep seated anxiety about the effects of the chemotherapy I was to undergo. Only a few knew that I had cancer, just our closest friends and our most senior and trusted management. The staff were unaware, and those with whom we were in business contact, bank managers and the like, knew I had not been well but they most certainly did not know the reason for my illness. If the bank manager can be a cad and a bully to his fit customers, think of the havoc he could create with a terminally sick one! I needed, with Wendy, to be out of the public view if the hair was to fall out or I was to become increasingly disabled and sick. I needed to protect our businesses and our employees from the vultures who would prey if they knew what we knew. Perhaps even more importantly, I knew I did not want sympathy. I did not want people to see me going downhill, thus the offer of the flat in Oxford was even more of a Godsend than might normally be imagined.

Though Mary's staff were downstairs they were all far too well behaved to impinge their sympathy upon me, and when Mary herself was there I would occasionally invade her inner sanctum and interrupt her busy schedule. She was a huge moral support to us and did much to boost our confidence in the future..

Confidence Follows

Three weeks after the start of the chemotherapy treatment we moved into Oxford and I attended my first dose of radiotherapy. Again, I'd been told to expect nausea, loss of appetite, skin burns etc.

We had decided to try to get the first appointment each morning, 8.00am. The reasoning was varied but pertinent in all respects. The first appointment was unlikely to be delayed due to the appointments book running late, so that to turn up on time or before should mean no prolonged wait for the treatment. The traffic in the city would not have built up to chaotic proportions as early as this, and finally it left the rest of the day free to attend to the business or rest or both. I'd been told by my medicine man that I should rest as much as possible to enable the body to fight the disease and not tiredness. His diet was aimed at the same conclusion, eat simple, easily digested foods so that the body's energy could be available to fight the tumour.

The first dose of radiotherapy was painless, unexciting and while it was frightening maybe to be left in a room with a vast gadget making funny noises, it was less traumatic than I'd thought. Anyway I was beginning to feel my confidence return since even as early as this in the treatment, even before the radiotherapy had been brought into play, there seemed to be that conspicuous improvement in the bladder. I was going as often, but that awful 'no go' situation that prevailed when I felt the urge to pee seemed a little better. It may have been wishful thinking but I thought I noticed that now, even with a slight urge, the bladder did in fact empty immediately, as opposed to having to wait for the urge to pass before being able to perform at all. There was certainly a change, and I believed a change for the better.

My blood count gained in strength. My appetite continued unabated. With an effort I was able to walk with less of a limp for short distances, albeit with the help of a stick. I found I could lie on my back without pain. The bladder allowed me greater lengths of sound sleep at night. My blood pressure began to drop. My bowel began to work as it had never before worked, the timing was often inappropriate but it worked. My eyesight improved. Rather than a trickle I was beginning to be able to pass water with a flow, though not equalling the horizontal drive of a ten year old, it was to me impressive - I could now comfortably clear the toecaps!

Then the burns started, small and, at first, not too distressing. I asked for something to put on them and was given hydrocortisone cream. If my head had been more streamlined I'd have reached the moon, such was the ferocity of pain when the ointment was applied. I rang my Chinese medicine man. I collected two aloe vera leaves and some aloe vera gel. I anointed myself with the leaf, instant release from pain and each application to the various bits brought about a cool and soothing relief.

My consultant examined me and reported back to my doctor that he had a certain sympathy for the patient with the sore bottom. My oncologist examined me and was openly surprised that the burns were nothing like as bad as he'd expected. I continued to draw upon the dwindling supply of aloe vera leaves and lavished their cooling interior to my poor sore bottom which, though I couldn't see it, I assumed resembled that of a baboon.

I had been prescribed 25 doses of radiotherapy, 5 days a week for 5 weeks. Each one was to take place at 8.00am and each one consisted of three different angles of penetration lasting in total for no more than 15 minutes. So at this early stage I felt nothing and merely entered upon a routine of counting, so that I knew roughly how long I'd been lying still. While I had an indelible ink mark on each buttock and had to lie face down, which was a blessing for the pain threshold, there seemed not too great attention paid to exact positioning each time, though I'm sure the team of nurses worked to a tolerance. My attendance was at the appointed time for each week day, excepting when the machine was out of action through breakdown or service which seemed to be once a fortnight. So the 25 treatments would take 6 weeks.

Weekends were for recovering, for as the treatment persisted so I became more and more tired. I would get back to the flat and while Wendy parked the car to evade the traffic warden, I would hobble to the bread shop outside our door, buy breakfast and then hobble upstairs. After my vitamins and blood pressure pills, after my morphine pain killers and after my decoction I would go to bed for several hours' sleep, getting up in time to have lunch before returning for more sleep. This routine was interrupted only when I had an essential business meeting, and those were put off or delayed whenever possible.

I would see the oncologist every two weeks and by the end of the fourth week it was quite clear that things were improving. Yes, the gut was taking a terrible pounding, I was eating less roughage and had little time to get to a lavatory if I didn't want to become extremely dirty. This was due to both chemotherapy and radiotherapy but the symptoms were definitely easing. The pain was becoming less, the bladder was beginning to become markedly better and with an effort I could walk with less of a limp. Hope was becoming a reality, though the doctors were constantly making small remarks that did nothing to inspire confidence. My medicine man, however, was a tower of strength and encouragement and I endeavoured to make an appointment with him immediately after my appointment with the oncologist on the same day, so that when the latter undermined hope the former could reinstate it with his positive approach. He always did, but I went from low to high and back to low again very quickly with the slightest provocation of either pain or negative statement.

Such statements being made by the Western medicine people whose job it was, I believed, to boost confidence rather than remove it. I suppose that they still regarded my life expectancy to be limited, and saw no reason to change either their views or mine. Certainly at the very mention of TCM, they all to a man showed that they held absolutely no confidence in it whatsoever, even to the degree of dismissal. Indeed, when in answer to the question asked how my bowels were behaving and my reply being 'irregular' to a man they all said, "What can you expect if you eat all those vegetables?" When told by the oncologist that my burns were looking better than he expected, the hydrocortisone cream he'd prescribed must be working well. I was glad to be able to say that I wasn't using his cream because it caused me too great a pain, but rather I was using the juice from an aloe vera leaf, and I was delighted that he felt it was obviously having such beneficial effect. Sadly, he wasn't remotely interested in the treatment I'd been prescribed by another, but he did say that in view of the way my body was standing up to the radiotherapy, he thought it might be safe to increase the number of doses from 25 to 33. So, though he'd not admit the reason why my body was faring better than he had originally thought, at least he agreed that I was able to take more treatment. That had to be a bonus. It is of course always possible that it was my body responding without the aid of either the aloe vera or my 'brew', but there is no doubt in my mind which it was, there is no doubt either that the cream hurt like hell while the juice soothed instantaneously.

As the treatment went on so the burns increased and so my lethargy at wishing more treatment increased, but I knew that I must endure it to the end. The actual treatment now hurt, I don't believe it was imagination. As the machine bombarded me, I was aware of being burnt where I was already burnt, not much of a sensation but sensation there was.

All this time I was still receiving continuous chemotherapy, so that the two treatments were running concurrently. The bowel was awful, constantly wanting to leap into action as often as I would let it, but the bottom was dreadfully sore with burns and constant wiping. One day Wendy appeared with a packet of 'baby wipes', the soft impregnated tissues with which one cleans babies' bottoms. I took to them with alacrity. Not only did they cleanse gently, they soothed as well, and after a time I smelt as a baby would from continuous use of wipes and cotton wool. Aloe vera leaves were also consumed at a prodigious rate, they continued to soothe greatly the areas of burn.

Meanwhile my good doctor was continuing to monitor my blood pressure on a regular basis and concluded that I might abandon my daily intake of beta blockers. My blood pressure had continued to fall, despite my mental anxiety and physical stress, and the fact that I was still on the receiving end of the radiotherapy and chemotherapy treatment. He could offer no clinical explanation for this, yet dismissed my suggestion that it could perhaps be because I was still sticking relentlessly to my diet, my vitamins and my Chinese herbal brew, and thus my whole system might be reverting to normal. Except the bowel of course, but Western medicine's dismissive response to that was to blame my excessive intake of roughage!

My blood pressure had reduced to 130 over 80. My white cell count was 6 plus. With the regular application of aloe vera I was able, just, to live with the burns and I was determined that I should sustain the increased amount of radiotherapy treatments that the oncologist had proposed. If, as I firmly believed to be the case, the chemotherapy and radiotherapy were working together to 'kill' the tumour, then the more treatment my body could take, the better chance they had. And if TCM was what was enabling my body to withstand more Western chemical drugs and radio treatment than expected, and I firmly believed that too, then truly it could be said that the treatments were complementary.

The final radiotherapy session eventually arrived, 33 treatments completed. But I was much, much better, so long as you ignored the bottom end.

I couldn't go without a stick but I could now go maybe 100 paces before I had to rest, and then more from fatigue than pain. I could actually stride out a little without pain in the hip, but I was still taking a considerable daily dose of morphine. Pill taking each day was now a constant but even if the quantity of pills was still vast, I was no longer having my prescription constantly changed. The nights were better too. I was only getting up maybe four or five times instead of every half hour as before. So steady progress was, I believed, being made and my medicine man was very pleased with the way my body was reacting to being poisoned and burned. He still only examined my tongue and took my pulses, but he pronounced the tongue to be in better shape, as were my pulse rates and my skin was clearer too, all good signs he said. He was a tower of psychological strength at the same time, constantly telling me how well I was doing and that there was an increasing hope factor that increased as I got better.

He never once let me believe that I was going to do anything other than get better. Rather a different approach from that taken by both my doctor and the oncologist, who would independently say good things to encourage and then meter the hope factor generated by continuing to cast doubt for the future, so that I never or seldom left them without feeling depressed. I believe their meaning was clear: "You're doing well, well done, but don't get confident because the improvement is probably only temporary". Temporary is impossible to define. Indeed there have been many words written which baldly suggest that it is pointless to bother with chemotherapy treatment at all, it can only prolong life sometimes by merely weeks, it seldom cures or prolongs life for a significant term. This attitude is one of defeat and should be kept away from patients who are trying to beat the disease, and it should not form part of the initial discussion, for there must be many who say "OK, that's it" and lose the will to live, having been apparently faced with certain death, especially when, if, as in my case, the prognostication comes in a characterless dingy room with nothing to lighten the spirit. Not fair whatever the prognosis.

So my Chinaman was an essential ray of light on my horizon at all times and remains so to this day. He is also a tireless confidante to both Wendy and myself, no matter how silly the worry, we can talk it through rationally with one who treats it with humour, wisdom, rationale and above all, hope.

John Cook

A Healer and Partial Return to Fun

While I was undergoing the height of radiotherapy treatment and we were staying in Mary's flat, she had a man on her staff who claimed that he was a 'healer', and would like to try and see if there was anything in his powers that would help me. Game for anything at that stage, I accepted his offer.

When first he came I was unable to sit for long, so while I lay supine on the bed he would pass his hands through the air just above my body in stroking motions, sweeping from the top of the body down to the feet. I did not tell him on the first occasion where the tumour was. He found it, he located it by heat which he said he could feel. I've no reason to doubt his statement and he could certainly not have known exactly where it lay by any other means than his own self discovery.

He continued to pass his hands above me from head to toe. Neither of us spoke. I began to have a very distinct feeling of heat in my left hip which he, with still no words passing between us, proceeded to 'draw' down the length of my left leg. I was aware of the passage of heat from hip to ankle. When he had finished he asked me if I had felt anything. I told him of the passage of the heat which seemed to have moved down my left leg. He told me that he had located heat in the left side and had 'removed' it down the left leg. He had found no other heat in the body so he had assumed that this must have been the problem area.

Interestingly, my left ankle became quite swollen and puffy for several days after that first treatment. He continued to 'treat' me, once or twice a week depending on his schedule, each successive treatment produced a similar experience of heat being drawn down the body, though never to the same extent as that first time.

I reported my experience to my medicine man, who was deeply interested. I never mentioned it to the doctors for what would have been the point? For myself I am fairly convinced that the tumour responded in some way to his methods, perhaps yet another complementary scenario which has helped to weaken the tumour's hold.

Towards the end of my radiotherapy, and while we were still living in Mary's Oxford flat, one of our horses was entered to run in a race at Market Rasen. We looked on the map, it was a long journey, far beyond anything that I would have contemplated in the preceding months. But I wanted to go. I resolved to give it a try. During the two or three days preceding the race, my mind and my determination fluctuated from one extreme to the other. One minute I would be going, the next I couldn't contemplate the thought.

So we planned; we tried to plan for every eventuality, including identifying hotels en route where I could be left for the day if it all proved too much. Wendy filled a plastic bag with baby wipes, spare nappies and other necessary adjuncts. She is not averse to remarking even now that travelling with me is worse than catering for a baby! We loaded my daily pill supply, Wendy spoke to the racecourse and arranged for a suitable meal to be supplied. We were off! For a day out! With fingers crossed the miles went by. It was a very long way, but we made it. The racecourse did us proud, with a restaurant table at which I could sit all day and see the action, if I did not feel able to peregrinate from stands to paddock and back.

On one of many trips to the gentlemen's lavatories, complete with carrier bag, I encountered one of our trainers, for whom the large bag caused lifted eyebrows and mild amusement, heaven only knows what he thought it might contain!

The day passed. I was able slowly to do all those things I wanted to do; to watch the horse being saddled, the jockey being put up, and getting to the stands in time to watch the actual race - just! Our trainer and his Kiwi fiancée were wonderfully supportive, with them on one side and Wendy on the other, I hobbled determinedly through the day, a day I shall always remember as the first of many signalling a gradual return to normality.

Unfortunately, the horse didn't appreciate that if he had put his best foot forward and won - or even managed to get placed - it would have put the icing on a very good day's cake!

John Cook

To France and Escape

When the radiotherapy finished it was decided that I should have a break from the chemotherapy too, to give the body a better chance of healing the burns quickly. I was detached from the tube for a month, two weeks of which were spent at home nursing my sores and two were spent at our home in France.

I felt I had been given a reprieve. Of course I didn't know whether I'd live for a year, and I had no idea whether I'd see France again in the autumn. Was this the last time I'd watch Portsmouth and England disappear into the night? My last view of Ryde church floodlit against the sky? The last time I would wander along the Canal du Midi under the plane trees?

But this was a real break. I was alive, with no pain, fewer pills and an element of hope gained, a good cocktail for a light-hearted few days of relaxation and pleasure. I still couldn't drive, so I sat in the car while Wendy drove us gently down through France, and we had a wonderfully carefree break in a delightful country; one we know well and which supplies proper food. Restaurants couldn't have been happier at being asked to deal with my dietary regime and the fresh vegetables and fruit in France are always so much better than those that can be bought in England.

A marvellous two weeks crowned by the discovery that I could map read without glasses. My eye sight was better. My doctor still argues that there is no clinical explanation for the fact. That doesn't seem to be particularly relevant in my view, the fact is that my sight is better. If someone says that there is no clinical explanation, it must be that he cannot see a clinical reason. In other words, something has happened about which doctors don't understand. Their problem not mine. Don't condemn the fact because you can't understand it! My medicine man on the other hand says the explanation is simple. The body is working properly, all the organs are in tune and the result is that the blood is cleaner and the state of one's eyesight is directly affected by the blood and its cleanliness.

I had established two facts; one that Western medicine is fallible in its lack of understanding and, more pertinently perhaps, does not appear to be interested in trying to understand and secondly, that Eastern medicine works in ways which are an anathema to most Western doctors. I'm not able to argue the logic of either, but I do know that my eye sight deteriorated and then improved and I do know that the improvement is still present.

I still don't need glasses to read where 14 months ago I could read nothing without them. I'll buy the medicine man's theory in the absence of another!!

With the help of the juice from the aloe vera plant the radiation burns, which had reached unpleasant proportions, soon became a thing of the past. By the time we returned to the UK the body felt fit to resume the chemotherapy blast which the oncologist said would now continue for an indefinite period.

We duly dragged ourselves back to England, where I was immediately reconnected to chemo tube and appropriately 'reholstered'. We settled into the weekly routine of a visit to the local surgery where the stalwart Jane, our district nurse, flushed out the line, changed my tube and made so many cheerfully encouraging noises that I looked forward to the occasion. My doctor, though still doubtful of TCM, became more accustomed to the fact that he was only in charge of a bit of my medication and he no longer had the lion's share of my faith; that had been transferred. So each week he took my blood pressure, which was my personal barometer of how I was faring, and also a blood sample to see how the body was coping with the chemicals. We compared the preceding week's levels with the one before so that at the least it was possible to determine that while the chemotherapy was working on the body and hopefully on the tumour cells, it was not having a detrimental effect on the system as a whole. Something that I had been assured would be bound to happen. But the white cell count remained high, the hair stayed on the head, and the blood pressure remained at a comfortably constant level. Was this due to TCM and its inherent ability to strengthen the body to resist attack? I believe so, and nobody in Western medicine has so far argued logically against that, though many have tried!

The effects of the chemotherapy were not startling, a few mouth ulcers which quickly departed. Otherwise, apart from the inconvenience of carting around the Baxter infuser and regular tube changes, the weeks went steadily by with merely a fortnightly visit to the oncologist and a three weekly visit to my Chinese medicine man. The former was perhaps becoming more hopeful though not exactly effusive, the latter was confident and his confidence continued to give me strength and hope, though I still had deep black mental patches when I would contemplate whether I'd ever see another winter, and all thoughts were deeply pessimistic.

External examination seemed to point to the fact that the tumour had become softer and smaller. Certainly, apart from a very weak and wasted left leg, all systems were more or less normal other than the ongoing upset to the bowel caused by the chemotherapy. I invested in an exercise bicycle and set out to rebuild the left leg to match the right so that I could once again walk without a limp.

Towards the end of January I had a further MRI scan. The tumour was smaller, might be haemorrhaging internally, but still covered over half the pelvis. It is perhaps an apt moment to recall that at first I was told I had a tumour the size of a golf ball, now it's rather bigger even though smaller! My doctor likened the result to an army camp after all the inmates had gone, the oncologist was pleased that the treatment appeared to be going well. Primarily I felt so much better despite the constant drip feed of the chemotherapy, and to all intents I was leading a normal life again.

In February I asked if I might have a few weeks off chemo while I went to France. The oncologist felt that this would be unwise, but when he found that I was determined to go to France, he suggested that I take a supply of tubes with me and make arrangements for them to be changed by a local doctor in the village. He proposed that I meet with the dispensing chemist at the Churchill, since there might be a problem with the supply of chemo in Baxters' tubes. We had continued to experience problems with every batch we collected. Often the tubes supplied by the hospital were incorrectly filled and my staunch ally, the district nurse, would frequently have to return them as unfit for use. Much interdepartmental wrangling ensued on each occasion: and the paperwork involved was staggering!

Before the scheduled meeting with the chemist, I was told that I could no longer expect Baxters' infusions since the hospital was no longer prepared to supply them. I had got used to the infuser and found it to be an efficient means of receiving the drug in an inconspicuous way. The system worked, I did not wish to change it. Meetings could be attended without electric motors, pumps and wiring, and the 'holster' rendered the Baxter tube, worn adjacent to the Hickman line, totally inconspicuous. I believed that any hint of illness might be detrimental to our businesses. Like many others, we were working hard to dig ourselves out of the dark ages of the early 90's. If I had told my banker that I'd got cancer and had been given a year to live seven months previously, I don't doubt that he, along with many others, would have made life for me more difficult. I cannot imagine that he would have smoothed my path! A sad reflection upon modern business ethics.

Since the hospital pharmacy and the oncologist were adamant that I must change to a different system, I decided to contact Baxters direct. They could not have been more helpful and agreed to provide me with what I wanted. The oncologist, realising that I was not prepared to be diverted from my course, reluctantly agreed to seek an alternative supplier of the drug for the same infuser. He knew that if he didn't, I would obtain treatment from elsewhere. When the first of the new supply was delivered, the irrefutable incompetence of the hospital's pharmacy was then convincingly proved since the new supplies were faultless, none having to be returned at all. The only problem was that they could not immediately provide the supply at short notice, so I had to come off the chemo for a few days. The oncologist pronounced this to be no problem, an interesting statement from one who only a few weeks previously had emphatically said that an interruption in treatment would not be beneficial!

I was becoming increasingly uneasy about the oncologist under whose care I had put myself. I'd had to bully him by fax in the first instance to get the treatment started; I had to threaten him when the hospital would not provide the Baxter treatment I required; now he seemed to have no clear idea as to how long he would continue the treatment and he had given me contradictory advice about an interruption in the chemotherapy. Was I confident that I was in the right hands and receiving the best treatment? I resolved to ask my GP to find another oncologist so that I might obtain a second opinion on my treatment to date, this would also provide a back-up contact should things not go forward as well as they had been up to this point with the existing treatment.

By April I was experiencing very sore feet, on some days it was painful to walk at all. To combat the problem I acquired from Duckers of Oxford, my cobbler of many years standing, a pair of very thick soled shoes. I had started chemotherapy in September and apart from a break in November / December of a little under a month to allow the radiotherapy burns to heal, and the few days' break during the change of supplier of the Baxters' infuser, my body had been absorbing a steady inflow of 5FU for the best part of eight months. Other symptoms included severe thickening of the skin on the hands and a loss of feeling in the fingers; an inability to put feet or hands in hot water without pain; a constantly runny nose and bloody stools. The bowel was also fairly erratic. My scalp had eczema which I controlled by washing my hair weekly with olive oil based shampoo. The feet and hands were kept moist by using Vitamin E cream.

But I was still alive and the worst symptoms of the tumour had gone, so the side effects of the chemotherapy were a small price to pay for life and hope.

During all this time my Chinese medicine man maintained my herbal brew and kept emanating confidence for me to boost my spirits. My blood count remained between 4 and 6 and my eyesight maintained the improvement I had noticed during our trip to France in December. My blood pressure remained constantly within normal tolerances without the need for formal medication of any kind. Indeed, apart from chemotherapy I was no longer taking Western medicine of any kind, no morphine, no beta blockers, no pain killers - just my Chinese herbs and the substantial daily intake of vitamins.

The sore feet would become less sore for a few days and then revert to being most uncomfortable. My hands, however, became more and more callused and swollen around the joints, particularly of the thumbs and at the wrist. The feeling in them also deteriorated to the point at which it became extremely difficult to do up buttons. By the end of April the mouth ulcers, which until then had come and gone over a day or so, were lasting ten days or so and becoming a great deal more sore.

The next MRI scan in April, which we had awaited with apprehension, showed a further considerable reduction in the size of the tumour and a still clear liver, or so it was said at the time. At my next meeting with the oncologist all was deemed very well, and it was decided that perhaps a further short break from chemotherapy could take place towards the end of May, while we went back to France to give the system time to recharge. There was still no policy for the future of existing treatment. I was however told that I could not expect my feet and hands to improve quickly at the cessation of chemotherapy. The effects would take a long time to withdraw from the system. A small confidence booster, and again the sort of hope damning comment that I had come to expect.

Within a few minutes of returning home from this morale boosting appointment the telephone rang. It was the oncologist, he had just been reviewing the MRI scan, which he'd had for at least a week before my consultation, and there was cause for concern.

The scan showed a shadow on the liver, it was perhaps unimportant but he had taken the precaution of making an appointment three days hence for me to have an ultrasound scan. I feared the worst, despite feeling so much better in myself, I became convinced that all was now lost. Wendy and I spent a miserable three days, finally the time had crawled by, we attended the hospital and waited in gloomy silence. The ultrasound machine was set up, its whirling and rotating pictures too technical for us to separate good from bad. Finally the young doctor who was passing the apparatus over my stomach in steely silence pronounced that he could find nothing sinister in the liver area. The oncologist had agreed to attend this not insignificant moment. He did not. So he was not available to answer what I deemed an appalling travesty of job execution on his part. By not having properly studied the original scans which he had had for ten days prior to my consultation, he had invoked needless worry and stress. I wrote to him accordingly.

My appointment in London with the second opinion came and went. Again, not a great confidence booster but I was at least told I was doing very well, though the treatment I had been having was not precisely what he would have himself prescribed. However, generally speaking what I had been given was good, and my overall reaction was satisfactory. I don't know what I had been expecting from this visit, but we left with a feeling of anticlimax, perhaps we had been expecting him to come forward with an instant 'miracle' cure. I do, though, remember coming away with the marked comparison between the ambience of the Royal Marsden and that of the Churchill indelibly printed on my mind. The former a quietly confident atmosphere of calm, the Churchill always giving out a feeling of technically necessary activity, unsupported by any attempt to tranquilise or comfort the spirit.

I was severed yet again from my tube, and spent two weeks recuperating in England in May before going to France for a further two weeks. Within days of coming off the chemotherapy my feet were no longer sore and I could walk. By the time we'd got to our house in France most of the soles of the feet had peeled away, revealing new, pink skin beneath. My nose stopped running, the bowel became more regular and feeling started to return to the hands, though they remained callused. So much for not recovering quickly.

I could sleep at night. I could pass water by day. I could read without glasses and no longer had to carry them around with me. I could walk without my trusty stick, and without pain, though it is certain that the muscles remain stiff, the joint likewise, and the leg was generally not as good as it had once been. This however does not denigrate the fact that I could do things I'd not done for months. I could sleep, I could lie on my back when I felt inclined, and I could push the clutch pedal of a car again. I couldn't yet run, but generally the bodily systems felt that they were approaching normal again.

At the next appointment the oncologist again professed himself pleased with my progress. He was somewhat perplexed that I appeared so fit and looked so well, he acknowledged that there had been an enormous improvement in my general wellbeing. He was also able to tell me that the tumour was now softer than it had been.

The Future with Home Truths in Prospect

May 1996. Where we go from here only time will tell, but I firmly believe that the application of centuries' old Chinese medicine, combined with sensible eating and the confidence of mind generated from the 'complementary' scenario, working with the advanced technology of Western medicine, has to be the reason why, in my case particularly, I have come through the initial treatment well. I have been able to support more than had previously been believed, and my body has healed well during my reprieve.

I will go to the next stage of prolonged chemotherapy, which will presumably be required after my scan at the end of the month, filled with the confidence that with the help of diet and Chinese medicine, my body can cope and derive the most benefit possible from the scientific treatment available, maximising my chances of defeating the tumour and prolonging my life.

I believe it to be utterly wrong that anyone should pronounce the sort of judgement meted out in the first instance by the oncologist, even under pressure from the patient to put a timescale on the disease. They cannot and they should say so. I also believe it is wrong for those concerned with conventional medicine to dismiss any form of complementary scenario in their dealings with their patients. In my case I was encouraged to continue to eat what I chose, for in their eyes it would make no difference. It may not, in every case, but it is not their brief to disparage and belittle any kind of system that encourages self-help, for it is the knowledge that one can help oneself that is so deeply important psychologically to the healing process. To take a pill and to wait for it to cure the ill, as I know to my cost, gives no mental stimulant to the healing process, merely added despair when the pill fails to work.

I've been there, done that! If you feel that eating five pounds of carrots a day, or swinging from a beam, helps the cause, then I believe the patient should be, if not encouraged at least not dissuaded, from pursuing any course of action which makes him feel he is helping himself. I am absolutely certain that my weight loss and diet have made my body more efficient and better able to cope with whatever is hurled at it, be it disease or curative measure.

If it is clinically impossible to explain why the conventional treatment that I have been receiving, has cured me of high blood pressure and restored my eyesight, then surely it must be acknowledged that the only other explanation has to be diet or my Chinese brew or a mixture of the two, for it is quite certain that my way of life has not changed. I still run my international business in exactly the same way as I did before.

It is a strange anathema to me that when making business decisions one surrounds oneself only with those who tell you the truth, the whole truth and nothing but the truth. If they don't, they're fired; if they do, one can make one's decision based upon knowledge. When it comes to health, the patient is not allowed to make decisions relating to his life; he must merely accept what he is told, when he is told. I was told I only had a year to live.

The assumption must be that the patient will accept that fact and work within it. Thus, as a patient one is perforce basing one's decisions upon hypothesis rather than fact, and being denied any control over one's own destiny. I also suspect that as in my situation, one is only told what the profession believes one should be told and that information is hard to come by.

If there is a lesson to be learned then it must be to seek not only a cure for the symptom from the doctor and his associates, but also to seek complementary remedies from alternative sources for the cause of the problem. In my case, had I gone to my Chinese herbalist earlier he would no doubt have prevented the cause of my original cancer and prevented all the hassle, expense and doubt of longevity. I believe I know this to be true.

I do know that even with a tumour, even after having had ten inches of bowel removed and the rest burned up with radiotherapy, even though my whole body has been subjected to a slow poisoning with chemotherapy for nine months, I feel better now than I have at almost any time in my adult life. So clearly the body wanted to work, has always wanted to work, it has just been deprived of the harmony within itself that would enable it to work, for I did not know how to help it and my medical advisers didn't either. They only attacked symptoms as they occurred, with whatever chemicals were available to them, they'd no idea how to harmonise the body's own machinery. I may have been asked to stick out my tongue so that the doctor can look down my throat, he may have taken my pulse in conjunction with my blood pressure, but never with a view to the 'balancing' of the body which enables it to harmonise.

It is, I believe, important for the medical fraternity to look further than merely at the patient's symptoms. They need also to look to outside their own experience in their attempts to remedy the cause. Their blind faith in their own infallibility has to be tempered in time to come, by their patients' refusal to accept in blind faith the infallibility of their diagnosis.

By the end of May 1996, when we returned to the UK, the more lasting and visible effect of the chemotherapy was to be seen in the nails of both fingers and toes. Not long after the cessation of chemotherapy in mid-April, it had become apparent that the nails had, in fact, not been growing properly. The existing nail was still fine and requiring to be cut, but as the weeks went by so the appearance of a 'joint' between old nail, 'chemotherapied' nail and new nail became evident. By July the old nail had fallen off the fingers, leaving behind an irregular, soft and flaky chemo'd nail, the top of which was some two thirds up where the nail might normally be expected to reach. The rest of the finger was nailless and until you're without a nail you don't appreciate quite what a useful bit of the body it is. No chance even of doing up the buttons of a shirt easily, for there is no rigidity in the end of the finger and you can't 'hook' the nail round the button as it emerges from the underside of the buttonhole! The effects gradually 'grew out', literally as the new healthy nail advanced to the end of the finger and the status quo was restored. The big toe nail took eight months to grow back, the fingers were fine four months after the end of the chemotherapy treatment.

The May scan showed no change. The oncologist pronounced himself well pleased and it was agreed that I should defer the next session of chemotherapy until the results of the next scan in August.

In August 1996 I was still sharing my body with my Hickman line, nearly a year since my oncologist had told me that I had but a year to live. The poignant words of Jaymee Bowen, the young cancer sufferer, in her television interview still ring in my ears from time to time, "While there's life, there's hope". Corny, I agree, especially when it comes from a young girl who should be able to see her life stretching out before her but acknowledges that she may not. Corny, maybe, but utterly relevant to every patient fighting every corner of the disease. I am still alive and after nearly nine months' chemotherapy, were it not for the doom, despondency and continual hope-crushing comments from the Western medical world, I would believe that I was cured and that life, the richer for the experience. I might go on as before, even in a better mode. Such is the experience of being told that death is ever present, that life, while there is life, is more greatly appreciated. Were it not for my Chinaman, who has done so much more than just administer herbs, perhaps the picture would now be very different and, as professed by the oncologist, I might indeed by now be a very sick man.

I'd been told that the line should stay in because the chemotherapy would be resumed at some stage. I assumed that this was because 'the course' had not been concluded. I did not question the motive. Foolish, for when in July I suggested that maybe the line might be removed for a while as it hadn't been used since April, I was told to expect regrowth of the tumour at any time, which would necessitate the reapplication of chemotherapy. This prospect had somehow escaped my otherwise fertile mind, so the new knowledge brought fresh anxiety. Was that new ache regrowth? Could it be that the hip was not quite so fluent of movement? Did I pee three times last night instead of once? All these questions suddenly took on a new and quite significant meaning. When my doctor said in response to my query on a new hip pain "Well, you're in Tiger Country now, you can expect regrowth at any time", I became obsessed with everything that might be construed as to pointing to not only regrowth but a new tumour somewhere else. "Wait until the next scan" I was told. "If the scan doesn't pick up either a liver problem or alteration of the existing tumour then we can remove the Hickman line. But be ready to replace it at short notice".

The August scan came. We waited with bated breath, every twinge, every odd ache had assumed gigantic proportions. We had no confidence in the outcome. "No change" was the immediate response. We breathed again. We took the decision and arranged for the line to be removed. It had caused me no physical problems during its stay. Its requirement for being flushed out and generally attended to on a regular basis had been an irritant rather than a worry, except when Wendy and I had been left to minister unto it ourselves, when it had become a major military exercise in cleanliness and accuracy! But it would be good to lose the evidence of the need to force feed the body with abnormal substances - and wonderful to take a proper bath without fear of immersing three feet of plastic tube in the contaminated bath water!

Two little nurses in the JR relaxed the hypochondriac with their chat as the tube was literally cut out of the skin and then drawn out of the body - a foot or more of it! The skin was stitched and within the week we were where we wanted to be, well off English soil enjoying all that a working life in France has to offer. Not least of which was taking the shirt off in the autumn sun to allow the air to get at a skin, which had been regularly cleaned with chemicals in the surgery and at home, but had not had the benefit of a proper wash with soap and water and exposure to the elements for nigh on a year.

We had left the country for an indefinite stay in France. We were aware that if something occurred to create extended worry we'd return post haste to the UK, but the country, the climate and the work were all so much more enjoyable than in England, that to miss the chance of a spell without the tube and the need to clean it out twice a week was foolish.

So it seemed that despite the ever gloomy Western medicine men, my Chinaman and I, with not inconsiderable help from Wendy were going forward. The next scan was not to be until the end of November unless I felt the need to have one before, and that need would be defined by symptoms of any sort of a prolonged nature. Something that lasted or got worse over a period of maybe a week plus. My Chinaman was confident that this would not be, and despite living in 'Tiger Country', a phrase irrefutable bad taste which continues to haunt me, I began again to look for and grasp hope, and again, Jaymee Bowen's positivity of "While there's life, there's hope". This must be a fundamental base belief for all cancer patients, who may otherwise be persuaded that they are on a preordained countdown. They may be, but so is each and every one of us and the countdown need not be orchestrated by cancer's clock despite the beliefs of the Western medicine world and its indoctrination of society. Especially that part of society that has the misfortune to suffer both at the hands of the disease and the doom of medical prognostication.

The November scan came and went. As it drew nearer so I convinced myself that new pain was becoming prolonged. That there were symptoms pronouncing the correctness of the doctors, but still I took my decoction and listened to the words of wisdom from the East. When the scan was over and the tumour still unchanged there was a great relief and moments of pure joy and hope, the likes of which I suppose don't occur after adulthood succeeds childhood, when simple pleasures take on such disproportionately large euphoric feelings. We celebrated and with relief looked forward to life for the following weeks, each period of life contained by time until the next scan, might maybe continue to allow hope and expectation.

At the end of January 1997 the scan again showed no change. The oncologist was actually heard to say that since it was now three years since the original operation and eight months since the finish of chemotherapy (and being particularly careful not to refer to the fact that I was now four months late in dying!) there was now a reasonable clinical chance that the liver might not become infected, and that the tumour could remain dormant 'for a period'. Great words from a man who had, eighteen months earlier, downed all my hopeful arguments for life and prescribed death as the result of the disease within that time span. "No need", he said, "to have another scan for four months".

So back in France nearing the end of that four months, we wonder and hope for confirmation that the tumour is still inactive. There are moments when I believe that I am ill again but those moments, which are prolonged at times due to a symptom lasting for several days, are getting less frequent.

A good thing or a bad thing? When faced with death and when keyed up to fight, there must be some element within one's make-up which enables one to fight on. Time and its resultant complacency can dull the urge to fight, but hope cannot be allowed to be extinguished. There must be periods of rest when the body can expect to retrench and revitalise its will to live?

Three Years On...

July 1998: I take up my story briefly again. It is now nearly three years since I was given that sentence of a year's life expectancy.

I have, we have, 'lived' life to the full. We are still endeavouring to live as though today is the first day of the rest of our lives. We endeavour to make each day a good day - often difficult in England with its lethargy and congestion, lack of honour and integrity and appalling levels of service and achievement but when, as now, we are in France, we usually manage to achieve just that. Each day is a progressive day and, above all, each day is one that we may look back upon as a day well spent and a day enjoyed with achievement. 'Pas de probleme' is oft heard as opposed to "Yeah, well, the reason it hasn't happened is because .. " and the long line of blame starts to intrude upon one's good feelings as we stay in England.

John Cook

Two years ago we planned a trip to China to attend a symposium on Chinese medicine and to visit various hospitals across that vast country. It didn't happen and my Chinaman was happy for he said I was not strong enough. We planned a trip to New Zealand too, but again it has not taken place and again my Chinaman was not unhappy. I feel good, in many ways better than I did twenty years ago, though the thought of 'Tiger Country' still attacks me whenever I have an ache or pain or the imagination is allowed to wander.

I can see without glasses, though Wendy might sometimes disagree. I can walk many miles a day without limp or stick and I sleep at night, as well as most and better, much better, than I did two years ago. I continue with my diet, I continue with my decoction and I continue with my vitamins. I do not take Western medicine though I would, in certain instances, on the advice of my doctor provided I had the agreement of my medicine man.

Some months ago I got a kidney infection, I was worried that it might be a new growth but everybody told me that it was not, and so it proved. My doctor ordered a course of antibiotics, my Chinaman ordered cranberry juice and a decoction to be drunk every three hours. I didn't take the antibiotics but I followed my Chinaman's remedy, though he said that I should take the antibiotics if his prescription didn't work. The pain should cease or not get worse. The pain ceased. The two systems didn't get a chance to be complementary in that instance but I'd rather a drink than an antibiotic and

I'm glad that Western medicine is maybe acknowledging the existence of the East.

My notes and drafts of 'Cancer - A Strange Gift' have been committed to a 'job for the future' over the last two years. I wrote a detailed case history of my ordeal thinking I was to be a star turn at a conference on complementary therapies in Beijing in 1995, the trip we were advised not to make. Time has passed by, life has been lived. Consultations with Western and Eastern practitioners have come and gone. The 'cure', if that is what it is, continues and my now six monthly scans show no change to date. My oncologist said last month that he believed the tumour was harder and less 'knobbly': "Good signs", he said, and went on to infer that as the years went by it might shrink and become less knobbly still. What a change in outlook from the gloom of three short years ago! However, the doctor in charge of reading the scan, that same individual who first broke the news in such heartless fashion, is less encouraging. His cheering statement that he had never known a tumour the size of mine be so dormant for so long before regrowth occurred, serves to remind us both that we are in 'Tiger Country' still. But there will always be a pessimist among Western medicine men. My Chinaman, on the other hand, tells me that he is now treating me as a 'post cancer' patient.

Now, with the ongoing and unfaltering help of Wendy, without whom so little of what has happened could have been endured, and whose support has now extended to the diligent translation of my untidy scrawl into computerised type. We are between us getting the manuscript in order so that we may confront the publishing world in an endeavour to spread a message.

I feel the need to spread that message because of what has happened to me, and as a result of what has happened to me many others suffering from cancer have come to me for advice, solace, call it what you will. There is, therefore, presumably a need out there for those of us who are afflicted to take strength from those of us who, though afflicted, seem to be going on. Sadly, there are those with whom I have been privileged to talk whose luck has run out. There are others who, like me, take strength from living to live on, taking that strength from whatever corner, nook or cranny they can, and having that element of luck that others have not had.

I cannot profess to be cured, 'Tiger Country' will ever be with us. But I have learned that the year I was given is stretching, the bus that might have run me over hasn't.

Those that knew of our ordeal during the first year or so are few, and confined to those that are dear to us and should know, those with whom we work closely and ought to know and a handful of others. Some of these are fighting their own battles, for as time has gone on, word has got out. I imagine it had always got further than we had thought, but the longer I have gone on 'bucking the system', the more open we have become in talking to others who face similar problems.

I have been asked by one or two whether I've asked myself "Why me?", or looked at others and asked "Why me and not one of them?" For such a question to have been asked, it must be relevant to thinking, and I have given it thought and talked to Wendy about its relevance to life. The answer is always negative.

I have never asked "Why me?" and I have never wished my problem upon another as an alternative. What I have thought, however, is not so much "Why me?" but "How me?" And that is a more difficult question to answer. Have these ills been sent for me to learn from? Have they happened as a result of the negligence of others or the negligence of myself, or have they been sent because my time quite simply is up? I am far more intrigued, as a result of the experience, in what part fate played and I can find no answer to that. Why did I become ill? Has many answers from food intake to medicine, all of which I have aired in these pages. Why did the long arm of coincidence introduce Mary as a catalyst for us to become aware of my illness before it was too advanced? Why did the chain of life's events bring forth my medicine man? And why or for what purpose has my life been allowed to be prolonged after a finite span had been diagnosed? These are questions that I ponder greatly, and one of the results is to make me wish to help others by my experience, and to awaken them to awareness.

I cannot answer any of these questions from any definitive point of view. I can conjecture that had I not had blind faith in my doctor and his medicine, I would have tried TCM and self- help before and the body might have been enabled to resist the cancer. I can argue, and I do, that had my doctor and his medical world of learning not had blind faith in itself to the exclusion of complementary methods, then I and they might have been able to go down the road that I have gone down earlier, and what then might have been the outcome?

Totally unswerving faith in the infallibility of one's chosen course, to the exclusion of any ability to think laterally, must produce blinkered vision in any field, and must culminate in its own inherent limitations and consequent problems. This is proven to be true in all aspects of living. Why should the very basis of life be threatened by such blindness in its attitude to health matters?

Of one thing I am quite certain, as I sit in the sun in France in June 1998, nearly three years after being told that twelve months was a reasonable life expectancy. I have never in my life felt so well. I do not know for how long that state will last, but nor does anyone. I sometimes pee once or twice during the night, but will often sleep right through. I have an uncomfortable feeling in the hip from time to time, and am aware that there has been damage and erosion in the area if I do something foolish. To squat on a French style lavatory doesn't do it any favours. I can feel the damaged hip but not the other one, so, I needn't squat! If I lift heavy weights I can feel the result in muscle stiffness later but so what? Two years ago I was still hobbling along on a stick and only able to drive an automatic car. Now I can walk as fast as the best, and have just driven a manual car 600 miles in one day without problems.

I pay heed religiously and relentlessly to my diet and continue to take my herbal decoction twice a day. I also still consume substantial quantities of vitamins every day, well in excess of recommended dosage and at the same level as when my medicine man first put me on to them.

I have an occasional problem of will power when denying myself the pleasures of pork crackling, foie gras and the steak frites which was once my staple diet in France, and which I have now to watch Wendy tuck into with relish! But it is a small price to pay for extended life, and a very healthy life at that. I can taste the way I've never tasted before, everything I eat has flavour. I can smell as never before. My tongue is clean and my mouth has a pleasant taste. My pulse is normal and my blood pressure better than average for my age. I take no Western medicine, and have been clear of colds and flu for three winters. My digestive system works, and I rarely have stomach cramp or the pain which for years I endured regularly. I have taken to the Real Tennis court again, albeit only gentle games with those good friends who understand the problems that may arise from dashing about with a shortened stern tube, over which I cannot claim to have total control! I still use nappies for insurance purposes when out and about, the twin effects of radiotherapy burn and chemotherapy poisons on an already truncated length mean that it will probably never quite return to normal. But again, a small price to pay for life.

Now the biggest question is "Why?" It is clear that without surgery the cancer would have spread and been fatal. It is clear also that without radiotherapy and chemotherapy the tumour would have gone on increasing, and created such internal problems that life would have become unbearable. It would undoubtedly also have spread to other areas and organs, which again would assuredly have been terminal.

It is equally clear that my daily oriental decoction and a specified intake of vitamins has kept me free from normal ailments such as colds and flu. So it is not unreasonable to postulate that these 'complementary' methods of treatment of the body as a 'whole', have also enabled my body to support far greater doses of Western science's chemical and radiotherapy treatment than its experts had anticipated.

These experts wouldn't agree with the concept, of course. To a man they will all congratulate me on still being alive and well. To a man they say: "You look very well..whatever it is you're doing must suit you. So carry on doing it." And to a man they acquire a glazed and disinterested expression, when I attribute no small part of my wellbeing to the benefits of following TCM principles.

It is not right that they should blindly dismiss the possible benefits of the positive approach that complementary medicine can provide. Even if they refuse to acknowledge that any technical medical benefit can be derived, they have no right to ignore or deride the psychological benefits that may stem from such systems. I am in no doubt whatsoever that my medicine man gave me the will to live and the strength to fight. To fight the disease and to fight the belief engendered by Western medicine that the disease would win. It may yet win, in the end, but God willing it won't, and at least I have given the beast a battering on the way, and the personal satisfaction engendered by outliving the prognostications has buoyed me up still further.

I am happy in my own conviction that without the advent of TCM, I might by now be dead or very ill indeed. It is a strange feeling to sit and write these words, but I know that l owe a debt to the Eastern world and I know that that debt goes beyond a blind faith. It is an awakening to a whole new philosophy and outlook, upon the treatment of the whole fit and healthy body long before it becomes sick. It is an awareness that while Western medicine clearly has a significant part to play in making us well, it also plays a very real part in making us more ill than need be in the first place, simply because of its faith in itself and its exclusion of any other possible healing ends.

It may sound ridiculous to some to say that the faith healer of whom I wrote earlier played a part in my recovery, yet I was aware of the sensation in my leg as he worked. His hands did not touch any part of my body, yet his 'air strokes' made me feel that much of the malignancy within my body was being drawn down my leg and dissipated into the air. I may be open to ridicule for always carrying with me the crystal that he gave me, firmly lodged in the pocket nearest the tumour. Who can say what good it does? It can certainly not be said to do harm.

John Cook

Several times a day the presence of that crystal reminds me to focus my mind on the tumour and its eradication. To concentrate on willing it to gradually dwindle away, to force it to expunge itself from my body. It is proven (though not to dedicatedly sceptical medics), that such healing has taken place down the ages as a result of this kind of self-help. Why knock any method that by any means may result in an improving situation for the patient?

Of course there are quacks and charlatans out there, but there are an increasing number of information sources available. A patient should be encouraged to explore complementary therapies, if no greater benefit derives, he can at least feel that he has control over a small part of his destiny, rather than placing blind faith in the kill or cure approach of modern Western doctors.

If that patient chooses to place his total faith in one science, so be it. That is his choice but he should be able to do so voluntarily, and after due consideration, not through ignorance of the complementary scenarios that are available to him. We are all ignorant of the intricacies of modern medicine. I believe, therefore, that those who practise the science should not abuse the blind faith of the patient who comes to them for treatment, of whatever sort. Though this slim volume deals primarily with cancer, for obvious reasons, there are a myriad of other illnesses and diseases which can be mitigated by the possible benefits of complementary treatment. Any practitioner of any science must surely be guilty of failing to practice his life's vocation, which should be to ensure that the best is done by those who seek treatment in ignorance of the science to which they appeal, if he fails to acknowledge his own limitations. It is a brave person who categorically states, insists and believes that he and his science alone have the right to be omniscient.

If you happen to be Chinese, your medical file lives with you, and you take it with you when you go to consult your medicine man. His brief is to keep your body balanced, your ying and your yang in perfect harmony, and it is for this purpose that you visit him. If, as an Englishman, you arrive at your doctor's surgery to tell him that you are feeling pretty well OK, then you can be assured that a rebuke will follow for having wasted a busy person's time. You can be certain that your GP will not check you out on a regular basis for 'balancing' purposes, yet this is precisely what is available within the complementary sphere.

For many years now, Wendy and I have visited our chiropractor on a regular basis, every two or three months, for an 'overhaul'. He goes over us with a fine tooth comb, and even if there is nothing obviously adrift in terms of misalignment, he is able to 'balance' any disharmony he may find in the internal organs, gall bladder or spleen perhaps. If you contemplate it, every nerve end to every organ and part of the body travels down the spinal cord at some stage, so it makes perfect sense that any kind of imbalance in the spine, skull or jaw can affect the operation of one organ or another. This is another example, like the Chinese principle, of maintaining the balance within the body.

John Cook

My GP has never examined me for anything other than the ailment of the moment which has prompted me to attend his surgery. He does not have unlimited time, and I do not attend him on an 'overhaul' basis. So the comparison is invidious, if you like, but I reiterate the relief that the chiropractor was able to give to my bowel problems by gentle manipulation, without recourse to medication and conventional drugs.

Wendy also attends a reflexologist on a regular basis, the basis of their technique is closely allied to the acupuncture principle, in that all the body's organs have pressure points which when suitably attacked produce relief and, again, harmonious balance. Reflexology has also become an accepted method of pain relief in complementary terms, and many reflexologists give their time for free to hospices which care for the terminally ill.

The lesson I have learned from all this is what has prompted me to put pen to paper. I believe it to be a fundamental principle that all we basic mortals in the Western world should learn, and it is this:

Because we still have blind faith in what modern Western medicine can do for us, and because the modern Western medical practitioner has blind faith in the curative abilities of his own science, we do nothing until it is effectively too late. We do nothing until we have a symptom of sufficient severity to 'bother' the doctor; we then expect our health to be restored by whatever chemical treatment of the symptom he deems appropriate. It never occurs to us that we are in charge of our own health, that we can get on and take advice to keep our bodies balanced. No, we wait until a clear symptom of ill health forces us to take medical advice.

It is a fact that the Chinese doctor is paid only by his fit patients. They visit him regularly regardless of how they are feeling. The patient only stops paying the doctor when he gets ill. The rationale of that simple system is not too hard to follow. It must be assumed that the Chinese medical fraternity are not destitute, so either their patients look after themselves and are never ill, which is improbable, or more importantly, their abilities are able to limit the occasions when their patients fall ill enough to require Western medical attention.

I am of the belief that were we all to be brought up from the start with this outward and all embracing faith in the balance of the body, then we would from the first learn to eat properly, exercise properly and turn, as a dog does to grass, to the herbal need of the moment. We would regularly attend our herbal expert, and probably the chiropractor, the reflexologist and the faith healer as well. We would remain fit and well. Then, like the Chinese, our last resort would be the surgery and the drugs of Western medicine, not to be derided, but to be used appropriately when all else has failed.

To take the example of my recent kidney infection. The pain was intense, my GP prescribed a course of antibiotics, my medicine man a special herbal tea and an intake of cranberry juice as a diuretic. My GP dismissed the TCM treatment, while my medicine man told me that I was not to discount the possible use of the antibiotics prescribed if his treatment didn't cure the condition within five days. It did, so the antibiotics went back to the surgery. But a strange dichotomy, the wider ranging philosophy accepts the occasional need for chemical drugs, orthodox medicine does not wish to believe that 'alternative medicine' (for that is how they see it) can produce an effective replacement for their chemically based drugs, which are able in their turn to produce side effects of significant proportions.

I know which I'd rather have, and my blind faith in my GP has long since been superseded by a faith in what I see as complementary medicine, its preventatives and cures. I think that the critical word is 'complementary'. Almost every time one reads a newspaper article, or hears a member of the orthodox medical community talking about anything from acupuncture to ying and yang, they choose to use the word 'alternative'. Why should it be defined so? It isn't an either/or situation. Modern surgery and drug technology is progressing in leaps and bounds, there are cures today that did not exist ten years ago. Chinese medicine, or any form of alternative therapy, cannot be expected to achieve the spectacular results which are now to be acclaimed. Fine. But that does not preclude your average man from using the benefits of age-old herbal 'wizardry', to help his system benefit far more from the modern chemicals and surgical procedures that are now on offer.

My faith in modern medical science as a last resort has not diminished, nor should it for the reasons outlined above. But its own blind faith in itself must surely be tempered by experiences such as mine. I have a secondary tumour, which for reasons the radiographer was unable to explain, seems to be 'in remission'. Couldn't read without glasses, I now can. My blood pressure was due to hypertension and was beyond all acceptable limits. It is now within them without prescription. I am told there is no clinical explanation for either of these events.

As a result of the events of the last three years, I would like to pose just one question to the modern medical profession: Scientific medical research moves constantly forward in its search for new cures and new understanding. But why will it not acknowledge, at no research cost, that there are significant benefits to be had from an acknowledgement of the thousands of years of history that lie behind Eastern medical practice? And in this instance, can it afford to dismiss what I am trying to do to help myself and others from the historical basis of proven medical technology?

Faith - blind faith - should not be blind to such dismissal.

Appendices

John Cook

Appendix A: Chronological Symptoms

Dates	Symptoms	Medication Prescribed
1960's	Severe bouts of stomach pains. Diagnosed ulcers	Motipress Colofac
1970's	As above, but diagnosed colitis	
1980's	Symptoms continued. Haemorrhoids, Bleeding	Colpermin
1984	Investigative barium enema shows severe diverticulitis. Advised may require operation to remove part of lower bowel if condition deteriorates	Ciproxin
1990	Symptoms continue. More blood in stools. Test taken	
September 1993	Requested further bowel investigation. Endoscopy revealed cancer	

Cont /...

Dates	Symptoms	Medication Prescribed
December 1993	Anterior resection operation to remove section of lower bowel and primary tumour. Other polyps also removed.	
1994	Quarterly checks from surgeon. All OK	
February 1995	Headaches and sore hip reported. Investigation revealed high blood pressure which had previously been normal	Nifedepine. Atenolol
March 1995	Eye sight still deteriorating, hip becoming more painful. Blood pressure controlled but not reducing. Bladder becoming impossible - up every hour - little or no flow.	Ditrapan
		Cont / ...

John Cook

Dates	Symptoms	Medication Prescribed
April 1995	Symptoms getting worse. Blood pressure still controlled by pills. Physiotherapy for hip. Kidney check. Visit to surgeon for 3-monthly check-up fails to reveal tumour despite internal examination and full details of symptoms	
May 1995	CT scan of abdomen and head normal	
July 1995	Symptoms unbearable	
August 1995	Referred to neurologist, MRI scan arranged to check lower back for hip problems. Unable to walk without stick. Scan reveals pelvic floor tumour	
September 1995	Connected to 7-day continuous infusion of 5FU. Commenced Chinese herbal brew	
October 1995	33 dosages of radiotherapy	
December 1995	3 week break from chemotherapy to allow recuperation	**Cont / ...**

Dates	Symptoms	Medication Prescribed
January 1996	MRI scan shows slight reduction in tumour size	
	Reconnection to 5FU chemotherapy	
April 1996	MRI scan shows continued reduction in tumour	
May 1996	Disconnection from chemotherapy to allow recuperation	
August 1996	MRI scan shows no change to tumour dimension	
September 1996	Hickman line removed	

No further Western medicine of any sort

Appendix B: Diet Principles

Loading the system with carbohydrate and protein at the same time gives the body problems in trying to carry out two processes at the same time. It processes the carbohydrate first, because it finds that simpler and quicker, and the protein that is left behind is never completely converted and lies around in lumps.

The more and higher protein we consume, the less the body is able to cope with it. So the principle of the Hay diet is to separate the intake of carbohydrate and protein, and to limit the amount of high protein ingested.

Prohibited foods: (to limit protein) are:

Dairy products (goat and sheep in small quantities is OK, including yoghurt and soft cheese because the animal fat content is much lower); Eggs; Shellfish; Red meat and Offal (includes pork!); Peanuts! (other nuts are OK); Chocolate

Restricted foods: Beans (blow the bowel's mind if consumed in quantity!)

Drinks:

Off limits: White wine (acidity); Tea and Coffee (tannin and caffeine); All fizzy drinks (on the basis that our bodies spend their time getting rid of carbon dioxide, so don't make life more difficult .....)

Allowed:(with meals); Red wine, Cider , Beer

So, in terms of meals it's either:

A: Carbohydrate: bread - potato - rice - pasta - pizza + veg

or

B: Protein: chicken - turkey - guinea fowl - fish + veg

Fruit at all times

About the Author

My own career, spanning 50 years, has been as principle or seed corn investor within a broad spectrum of business opportunities worldwide. Involved initially in my family's farm in Gloucestershire in the 60's and most recently in a stem cell research spin-out from The Royal Veterinary College . Among other themes, I have farmed in New Zealand pioneering homeopathic medicine from deer velvet; helping the New Zealand government with efficient distribution of electricity within their Chatham Island protectorate and, in Australia, perfecting the collection of umbilically derived stem cells from horses. As well as farming and allied professions, I have been involved closer to home in general business endeavours including energy use and generation, and within the service and distribution sectors.

I am an ardent supporter of my old school, Malvern College and as a past president of the Oxford University Real Tennis Club, I have played Real Tennis for many years. Having stood for parliament as an independent in the 2010 General Election, I am extremely interested in the interactions between politics, economics and religion.

The End

Printed in Poland
by Amazon Fulfillment
Poland Sp. z o.o., Wrocław

60547928R00101